RAPID VIZ, THIRD EDITION
A NEW METHOD FOR THE
RAPID VISUALIZATION OF IDEAS

Kurt Hanks | Larry Belliston

Course Technology PTR
A part of Cengage Learning

COURSE TECHNOLOGY
CENGAGE Learning™

Australia, Brazil, Japan, Korea, Mexico, Singapore, Spain, United Kingdom, United States

COURSE TECHNOLOGY
CENGAGE Learning

Rapid Viz, Third Edition
A New Method for the
Rapid Visualization of Ideas

Publisher and General Manager, Thomson
Course Technology PTR: Stacy L. Hiquet

Associate Director of Marketing:
Sarah O'Donnell

Manager of Editorial Services: Heather
Talbot

Marketing Manager: Heather Hurley

Acquisitions Editor: Mitzi Koontz

Marketing Coordinator: Jordan Casey

Project and Copy Editor: Sandi Wilson

PTR Editorial Services Coordinator:
Elizabeth Furbish

Interior Layout Tech: Bill Hartman

Cover Designer: Mike Tanamachi

Proofreader: Sara Gullion

Special Consultant: Michael V. Lee

Visualizers: David Bartholomew, Scott Bevan,
Carl Haynie, Becky Miller, Stan Serr

For product information and technology assistance, contact us at
Cengage Learning Customer & Sales Support Center, 1-800-354-9706

For permission to use material from this text or product,
submit all requests online at **cengage.com/permissions**
Further permissions questions can be emailed to
permissionrequest@cengage.com

Sources for the illustrations accompanied by subscript numbers are listed in the Credits at the back of this book.

All other trademarks are the property of their respective owners.

Library of Congress Catalog Card Number: 2006900546

ISBN-13: 978-1-59863-268-2

ISBN-10: 1-59863-268-X

Course Technology
25 Thomson Place
Boston, MA 02210
USA

Cengage Learning is a leading provider of customized learning solutions with office locations around the globe, including Singapore, the United Kingdom, Australia, Mexico, Brazil, and Japan. Locate your local office at:
international.cengage.com/region

Cengage Learning products are represented in Canada by Nelson Education, Ltd.

For your lifelong learning solutions, visit
courseptr.com

Visit our corporate website at
cengage.com

Printed in United States of America
14 15 16 12 11 10

Contents

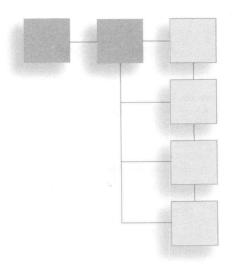

RAPID VIZ—NOT ANOTHER DRAWING BOOK

When I mentioned to an architect friend of mine that I was thinking of writing a book on drawing he just stared at me. Then he bellowed with hands waving in the air, "All we need is another drawing book. Why you could fill this room with those kinds of books. There are thousands of them covering everything you could possibly want to know about drawing." Then he pointedly asked, "Why on earth would you want to do another?"

It is a good question. Why would I want to do another? The answer comes from personal experience. It involves my own development; I want to explain to you what I feel drawing, thinking, and visualizing are all about.

My visual education began later in life than it does for most people. It began when I was in college. My only previous exposure was doodling on scraps of paper, around the borders of English themes, on the pages of the phone book, and other such random places. In college, I floated around various majors and finally landed in

design. In that college you had to learn to draw if you wanted to get your ideas across. Drawing was something you were made to learn—something you had to go through and get over like chicken pox. And so I did it. After taking several classes, putting forth considerable effort, and filling innumerable waste baskets with discarded drawings, I finally reached an acceptable level of proficiency. But the whole education process seemed too long and too involved and too filled with unnecessary and inefficient teaching for what I finally gained.

I realized, however, that something else had happened along the way. Yes, I had learned to draw, but more importantly, I learned to *think*. My whole method of thinking underwent a complete metamorphosis. I began to *see* the world more clearly. As my hand sketched the lines, my mind revealed a whole new method of thinking that I had not known before. Being able to visualize things gave me a tool that I could use in all facets of life. What happened to my mind was much more important than the sketches I produced.

Learning to use pen and paper had thus revealed talents I didn't know I had. Not the great talents of a fine *artist* in the traditional sense that you might expect, but I had discovered the important, practical ability to visualize. I gained the ability to picture something mentally, and then quickly convert those thoughts into visual reality on a piece of paper. I could nail down my ideas on a sheet of paper.

I realized that converting these ideas had to be a rapid process taking a minimum amount of time, trouble, and work. An idea is a very delicate and fleeting thing and if it is not quickly crystallized into reality, it just slips away never to be found again. A rapid conversion from thought to paper is critical.

I found myself asking the questions: Can this new-found skill be taught to others? And can it be done without all the hassle, redundancy, and expense that I had gone through in my own education?

As so often happens in life, I found myself regretting my former criticisms of teachers as I became a teacher. In a classroom situation I began to challenge students to learn the kind of drawing that had become such a valuable asset in my life.

For the next couple of years, my students and I developed a method that worked. The students helped me reduce drawing to the essentials. Instead of a fine art approach, we developed a simplified approach to drawing that people can use for thinking, learning, and communicating.

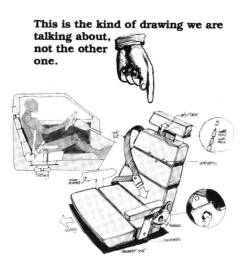

This is the kind of drawing we are talking about, not the other one.

This book is an outgrowth of classroom teaching. By trial and error we discovered the best teaching approach. I hope that you, too, will gain by the experience many students went through to develop this condensed teaching approach.

Earlier Education Can Hamper Our Thinking

Through my teaching I found that often the less you know about drawing the better off you are when learning to visualize. The less you know, the fewer preconceived ideas you have about drawing and visualizing. You have an advantage in that you do not have to unlearn what you already know. I can remember one class in particular in which I had two separate groups: one made up of architecture and landscape architecture students who had a lot of previous drawing experience, and another made up of beginning interior design students who had no experience (they had no idea what a "T square" was). At first the experienced group excelled over the inexperienced group. But the interior design students with no previous drawing experience just kept plod-ding along until, in the end, their performance actually exceeded the more experienced students' performance. I've found that experience often breeds indifference to what may seem to be simplistic and rudimentary exercises. But simplicity has an uncanny way of positioning itself behind genius.

About This Book

The objectives and guidelines used to develop this book were to:

- Produce a practical workbook to help individuals visualize their thoughts.
- Use examples and exercises that have been tried by students.
- Use tools, technology, and definitions that relate to a student's understanding.
- Design the content of the book for students and professionals in the fields of architecture, landscape architecture, engineering, industrial design, interior design, and other sciences and arts in which visualization is vital.
- Emphasize speed in mastering actions and concepts, reducing time, effort, and cost of learning.
- Use materials and equipment that are easily attainable and economical.

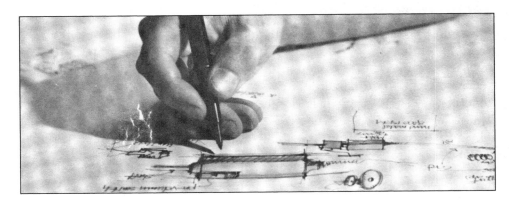

- Structure the information from simple to complex, from concrete to abstract, from general to specific.
- Apply visualization to real-life situations whenever possible.
- Provide positive reinforcement to students to prove that they *can* draw and visualize their own ideas.
- Have students learn by doing.

This last objective was especially important because while visualization is more a mental process than a physical one, the mental process is learned by actually doing.

Goals of the Rapid Viz Technique

I've found it easier to teach rapid visualization by starting in a logical sequential manner—the conventional teaching method. If a radical new concept like Rapid Viz is taught in a radical new way, people feel overwhelmed. By starting off teaching the Rapid Viz concepts in a conventional manner, students become comfortable with the techniques and slowly transition to intuitive learning.

The exercises that accompany each chapter may seem strange, but they have each been created and tested to be effective in reinforcing the techniques presented in the chapter text.

The Rapid Viz techniques featured in this book are designed to do the following:

1. To help you develop your own unique style of visual expression. This book is not designed to help you become a master illustrator, but rather a visual thinker and communicator. The exercises take you from copying someone else's visuals to making your own. As the book progresses, you should develop your own style that is comfortable and works for you.

2. To push your abilities. Improving your visual expression skills is a skill, and as such it requires practice. Just as a weight lifter improves his performance by lifting more weight and a runner improves her time by running faster or longer distances, you must push yourself to work faster in shorter periods of time to produce results.

3. To help you defer judgment. One of the most dangerous pitfalls of learning visual skills is the tendency to judge your work too soon. You may think that your drawings look silly at first, but keep working through the exercises and you will see progress.

4. To maintain your sense of humor. Many artists would turn up their noses at cartoons and nonsense doodles that are often featured in this book. However, if you can find the humor in your drawings, you can defer judgment and allow yourself to develop your skills. Taking things too seriously too early in the learning process discourages some would-be visual thinkers from developing their skills.

5. To set tight parameters. The exercises attempt to restrict your freedom temporarily. Tight restrictions as to what is to be drawn, how long to take, and so forth make drawing easier during the early stages of the learning process. Do the same for yourself. Set your own tight goals. Too many choices breed

confusion and non-performance. Decide specifically what to do and do it.

6. To reinforce that Rapid Viz is a progressive process. You will learn a little at a time. Go back over sections of the book to see your own improvement. Progress in small steps instead of trying to leap immediately to an end result.

7. To create a sequential learning system. Like many things, the Rapid Viz techniques are more easily learned after first mastering preparatory skills. Follow the order of this book so you can build upon the skills step by step.

8. To apply the techniques to a variety of scenarios. You may wonder why some exercises seem applicable only to a specific profession, such as architecture or city planning. The point of applying the techniques to areas beyond your own work or study is to reinforce that the principles are the same. When you learn by drawing objects outside your normal frame of reference or comfort zone, you will learn a great deal and avoid falling into old habits.

9. To keep a visual record of your progress. Save the drawings you create throughout this book. Record the date or sequence in which you created the drawings. When you go back to review your progress you will be amazed at how far you have come.

10. To provide an accessible teaching medium. I believe that a live teacher is the best way to learn the Rapid Viz techniques, but this book is the next best alternative when a live instructor is unavailable to you for whatever reason. The methods used in the book have been tested and improved through feedback from many years in a classroom environment. The self-study available in this book will require effort on your part, but the effort extended will be worth the rewards. Learning Rapid Viz will not only change your drawing abilities; it will expand your thinking abilities.

Another Way of Learning

There are at least two ways of learning and knowing something. One way is the traditional method taught in the educational system—reading, writing, and arithmetic. With this method you read something, you memorize it, and you are supposed to be able to recall what you learned.

There also are other ways to learn and know something. One way involves the "feeling" method in which you know something because you feel it. Drawing is more the feeling and intuitive kind of learning and knowing than it is the sequential, rote memorization method of learning. Drawing is much more dependent on the intuitive, creative side of the brain.

An example of "feeling" learning is when I learned to shoot a rifle at targets thrown into the air. As a youngster I took pride in my ability to shoot accurately. One day a friend and I went shooting together—he outclassed me terribly. He was a magnificent shot, and I wanted to be at least as good a shot as he was. I had learned about a method of shooting wherein you shot from the hip without taking aim. You aimed by "feel" rather than by looking down the sights of the gun. So I set out to learn this "feeling" method of shooting.

Another person would throw items into the air and I would shoot from the hip. It's like pointing your finger—you don't need to look down your finger to know that you are pointing in the right direction. As I became able to hit the thrown targets, I progressed to shooting them from a greater distance. Then I progressed to smaller and smaller targets until I became very proficient at shooting moving targets in the air.

With time and practice, I eventually became a very good shot by feel. You may assume that the best way to learn to shoot is by looking down the sights of a gun, but I actually became a better shot by feeling as opposed to the logical, traditional method. And wouldn't you know, my friend even improved his own already magnificent shooting ability by adopting the feeling method too.

Intuition vs. Logic

Another example of relying on feelings or intuition is speed reading. Conventional reading experts will tell you that it's impossible to read a book in 10 minutes and comprehend what you read. But some speed readers do it all the time and have better comprehension than regular slower readers.

What's their secret? They "feel" what they read. They give you correct answers because they feel the answers are right. They don't rely on logic and sequence to recall what they have read. Speed readers utilize the visual, intuitive, holistic half of their brains.

Visualization is to drawing as shooting by feeling is to feeling by sight. Visualization is to drawing as speed reading is to conventional reading.

Let me describe how the feeling method works in drawing. You know what perspective drawing is—it is when you draw things in three dimensions giving the appearance of distance and volume. The conventional method is a laborious method of connecting lines and projecting images. It is an elaborate method of drawing that is difficult to under-

stand, more difficult to learn, and extremely difficult to do well. It's no wonder many artists don't do perspective drawing.

A teacher once told me there is no other way to do perspective than by the conventional method. Wrong! The rapid visualization method is better and easier. To provide it, I have taken students that seemed to have equal abilities and taught one the traditional elaborate method and taught the other the rapid visualization method. Invariably, the rapid visualization method works better. The Rapid Viz student learns in a few minutes rather than a few hours. The end result also is unquestionably better than the work done by the student using the conventional method.

Getting the Most Out of This Book

Please do more than just read this book. If you only read and do no more, it won't work for you. The book must be used to be of any value to you. Write in it, draw in it, insert your own pages in it, and do whatever else seems helpful to you.

Far too often education becomes too restrictive, filled with constraints and negative comments. The only possible result is to make the student an outsider—a bystander looking in. But to really understand anything you must actually do it. Second-hand learning from someone else telling you about it never is very effective.

You can't learn to visualize by osmosis. Over the years I've had a lot of students who have tried. They seem afraid to fail; scared of criticism about their awkward sketches. But they—and you—should not let fear inhibit learning. Learning takes time, involves making mistakes, and involves effort. No one has learned to run without walking; no one has learned to visualize without drawing.

I hear and I forget.

I see and I remember.

I do and I understand.

—Chinese proverb

The brain is like a muscle that must be used. If not used, it atrophies and becomes weak and ineffective. With Rapid Visualization, the brain, in essence, becomes connected to the muscles in the hand. Coupled with the eye, the brain and hand muscles begin a continuous cycle of expression and feedback that enables you to transfer thoughts from your head to expressions on paper where they can be refined and recorded.

What I really want to encourage is your participation through your mind, your hand, and your eyes. All this participation is important because, as noted earlier, while drawing is more a mental process than a physical one, it is learned by physically doing. You have to push those thoughts out of your mind with a pencil, and then draw and develop them before your eyes on paper.

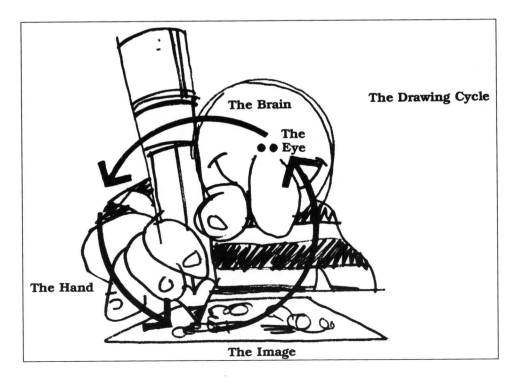

The Drawing Cycle

The Brain

The Eye

The Hand

The Image

Make this book yours. Force it to give you what you need. Don't separate yourself from your own education. By itself, this book is not the best method for learning—not as good as an interactive classroom situation—so you must force the book to fill your needs. You must take an active part in your own learning process.

In case you are wondering, my architect friend who expressed so much skepticism about this book eventually changed his mind. In fact, he helped refine and develop this book. There is a great need for Rapid Visualization in his profession as well as many others.

> I do not think that we have begun to scratch the surface of training in visualization.
>
> —Jerome S. Bruner,
> Educational Psychologist

What You Need to Get Started

A frightening thing awaits you. It has made strong men cry and sent women fleeing from its very presence. It is a blank piece of paper. What are you going to do with it? What threat lies beyond its snowy white innocence? You are going to have to make a mark on it—you are about to violate its purity. Can you do it? Of course you can!

First, you will need materials. You can play the game that some illustrators and designers play, which is to buy the "best of the best" exquisitely made and guaranteed for 40 years or 40,000 miles pen or you can simply buy a regular felt tip pen. I recommend that you choose the simple felt tip pen. It is cheap, easy to use, and always there when you need it. For now get any pen or pencil you can find. We'll have none of this "I can't go on with the work because my special order pen has not arrived yet from Walla Walla."

Use whatever you want as long as it's simple, cheap, and you can carry it in your pocket or purse at all times. Don't be one of those designers who is crippled without special drawing tools.

The kind of pen I prefer is a simple felt tip pen with a flexible point. Flair, EG, and Pentel (to name a few) make the inexpensive pens that I like. The only really important thing to me is that the point be able to draw thick lines when I press down firmly or thin lines when I use a light touch. Ball point pens don't allow this flexibility.

You may decide upon a pencil. I like drawing with pencils but prefer that you begin drawing with a pen. With a pencil you can easily erase and fix up rapid drawings. You should be learning to do rapid drawings correctly the first time, not learning to fix up your drawings. A pencil causes many people to become "fix up" artists. You need to be committed—once the pen makes a mark the deed is done. So, for now, use a pen; save the pencil for later.

When it comes time for the pencil, what pencil should you buy? Pencils are rated 6H (hard) to 6B (soft). If you like to scratch your message in the surface with a nail, then 6H is the pencil for you. If you are a real soft touch, then 6B is the one for you. For me, 2H feels right—not too hard, not too soft.

Also, you may want an eraser, in spite of my earlier remarks about erasing. To erase pen lines drawn with a felt tip pen, I wet the end of a pencil eraser. To erase pencil lines, I use a kneaded eraser.

You may want to keep a ruler handy as well as a variety of colors of felt tip pens. I find it fun to draw in black and then use some other color to add emphasis. The second color is my way of doodling with a drawing. You won't necessarily need these other colors or a straight edge, but you may find them fun and inspiring.

Remember that intimidating blank piece of paper? Well, obviously you will need paper to write on. In the beginning use the paper in this book. If the instructions are to complete an

Many people have the tendency to load themselves down with tools they cannot afford, cannot easily use, and don't really need.

exercise in this book, do it! Don't be afraid of ruining the book with your drawings. This book is designed to be used as a workbook. It's not a book to look pretty on your library bookshelf.

You'll need two other kinds of drawing paper as well. A good basic paper is regular bond paper—the kind you write on and type on. Most drawings will be done on cheap bond paper. You'll need tracing paper as well. In one part of this book we cover how to evolve drawings. To evolve a drawing

you will need to trace and refine your initial sketches. I prefer a 14" x 17" pad of tracing paper that is easy to see through but strong enough not to tear when you write on it. The least expensive paper you can buy that will do those things is the kind you should buy.

You need to get to know your pen so that it becomes an extension of your hand. Your pen becomes part of you. You need to become so familiar with it that you don't think about it. This comes from drawing or doodling a lot.

A tennis player's racket becomes an extension of the player's arm and hand. He automatically knows how far it will reach to hit the ball. Until a tennis player becomes one with his racket, he can't play tennis well. The way a player learns to control his racket is by hitting tennis balls. He doesn't jump right in and play a championship match with it the first time out. He just hits the ball over and over again at walls, fences, other players, whatever.

You are like the tennis player. You are trying to fuse your hand permanently to the pen. The way you do this is by drawing. Scribble and doodle often. Practice every chance you get.

The ultimate goal is to have the tools fuse with yourself.

Lines seem deceptively simple, but they are a critical drawing tool, and the first drawing technique you will learn. There's good reason for mastering lines:

- Line drawing is a quick way to visualize ideas with a minimum use of time and materials.

- Line drawing tools and materials are usually the easiest to use and the least expensive.

- Line drawing is the natural way to draw—children begin with line and adults usually continue with it as they doodle throughout life.

- Lines emphasize the basic structure and composition of a drawing, which ensures more probable success and a more effective sketch.

- Lines provide a framework on which to hang other drawing techniques such as shading and color.

- Lines are easy to reproduce on copy and blueprint machines.

Exercises

Now that you have the necessary tools, you are ready to begin. The first few exercises may seem a little too easy, but they are really the start of the learning process. The important thing is for you to begin doing something to get familiar with your pen and paper. Every exercise featured in this book has been created and tested to be effective in accomplishing a specific purpose or mastering a specific technique.

Exercise I.1

Start with lines. Make some lines with your pen—thick lines and thin lines. Try different pressures on the pen point. Lay the pen down on the paper; use the side of the pen tip to draw a line. Become familiar with the results you get from varying degrees of pressure and angles of the pen.

Exercise I.2

All of the drawings on this page were done with a single pen. These thick lines, thin lines, dark lines, light lines, crisp lines, and fuzzy lines are all a product of the same pen. You need to learn to control your pen to be able to extract the variety of lines shown in this example. Finish filling in the page with heads using various line qualities.

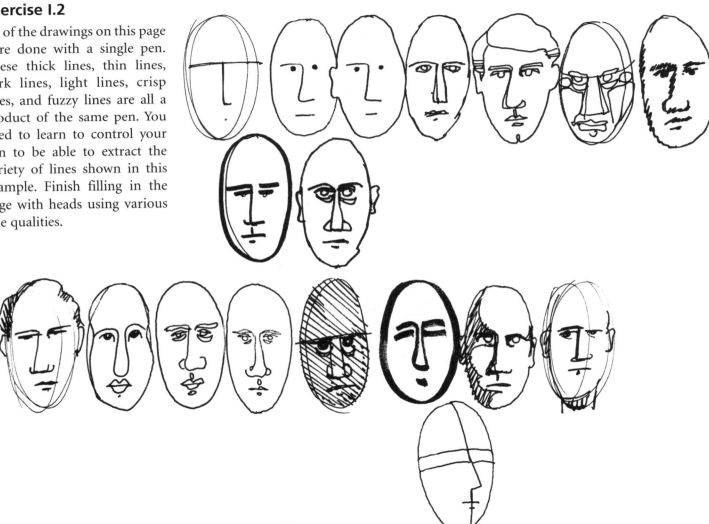

Exercise I.3

In an attempt to get your mind in the groove of thinking visually, draw your own simple doodle. Ask a friend to make something from the doodle. Here's an example of how it is done.

Now make something from your doodle. Quality of drawing is not an important consideration. Just make sure that your drawings are recognizable.

Exercise I.4

Look at the squares in the following image. These images represent:

a) early bird getting the worm

b) Custer's last stand

c) a flamingo swallowing a barbell

d) a man wearing a Mexican sombrero riding a bicycle

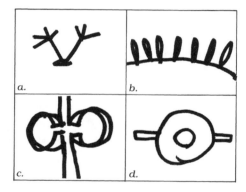

Following the style of this exercise, see if you can determine what the images below represent.

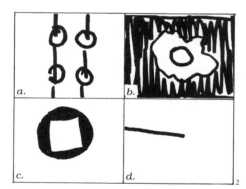

Answers to Exercise I.4:

a) a bear climbing a telephone pole

b) the view of the sun through a chuck hole

c) a square peg in a round hole

d) the end of the line

Exercise I.5

Using incomplete pictures as in Exercise I.4, depict the following things in the empty squares below.

  a) a porcupine's pillow

  b) Abraham Lincoln taking a bath

  c) a spider doing a handstand

  d) the other side of the argument

a.	b.
c.	d.

Exercise I.6

In the last empty squares make up your own visuals. (If you are tempted to skip this exercise, don't! Learning to think in visual patterns takes practice, and this is a fun, easy exercise. Just try it.)

a) _____

b) _____

c) _____

d) _____

a.	b.
c.	d.

Exercise I.7

We've all played the game of guessing what we see in puffy cloud formations in the sky. This next visual exercise is similar to that game. Instead of clouds, you will decide what you can "see" in the following squiggly lines and match each to the descriptions below. (Note: In some instances it isn't necessary that you see a distinct image in the line, you might just get a certain "feel" from the squiggles. There is no single correct answer. This is an intuitive exercise.)

- He had learned the amazing ability from his brother's dog.
- After laboring for weeks, she was ready for the unveiling.
- The weird Gopile stomped down Main Street consuming everything in its path.
- How long it had been there was impossible to determine.
- Maude had never been married; indeed, it was doubtful that she had even had a suitor in her 61 years.

Exercise I.8

Make up your own squiggles and sentences to describe what they represent. Remember, there is no single correct answer to this intuitive exercise.

a.   b.   c.   d.   e.

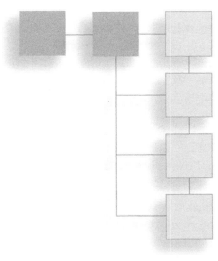

CHAPTER 1

PERSPECTIVE

One of the greatest challenges for people to learn is to draw in correct perspective. Teachers have struggled for years to find methods to teach students to draw correct perspective rapidly and easily. I have found a method that works well and is easy to learn. It will work every time. Even if you have no artistic training, this method will enable you to create drawings with accurate perspective.

The Box Method

The box method involves a box or cube. If you can draw a two-dimensional square correctly, you then can easily draw a box. If you can draw a box in accurate perspective, you can draw anything accurately and in perspective.

It sounds simple, doesn't it? It is simple. It will take some practice. It will take time to understand what is happening. You will have to practice those things mentioned in this book. But, if you do practice the method, you will find it is really quite easy.

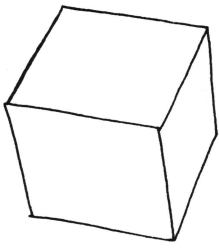

On the following page is a box that you must cut out. Do not be afraid—this book is meant to be used! Cut out that page and cut the figure to assemble the box as shown. You will need to tape or paste the edges together to hold the final box form in place. You will use this box to look at and draw in the upcoming exercises throughout this chapter.

Once you have assembled your box, you need to find a piece of clear glass or Plexiglas or vinyl (like a clear report cover) and a felt tip pen that you can use to draw on your clear piece of material.

This is what the assembled box should look like.

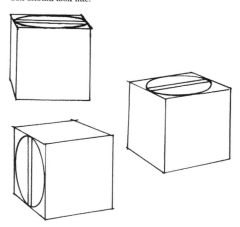

Take your box and set it up behind your clear material. Then hold the clear sheet stationary while you trace the box on it. Hold everything very steady. Trace the box exactly as you see it. Keep your eye in one steady position, the box steady, and the clear sheet still. If you don't move any of them, then you can draw the box in correct perspective.

Hint: Don't use both eyes. Shut one eye. If you use both eyes, you will get a double image making it difficult to draw.

Use only one eye

The Box
Clear Sheet

An Intelligent Individual Like Yourself

If you move the box up or down or if you move up or down, you will see different views, or planes, of the top and bottom of the box. The view of the surface that you see changes as your eye level changes. This eye level line is called the *horizon line*. The horizon line is always level and is always at the level of your eye. Thus, the view of the top and bottom of the box changes as you move your eye level or horizon line.

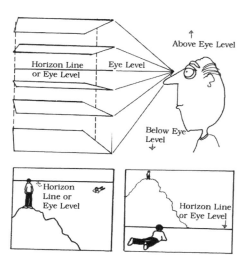

Above Eye Level

Horizon Line or Eye Level   Eye Level

Below Eye Level

Horizon Line or Eye Level

Horizon Line or Eye Level

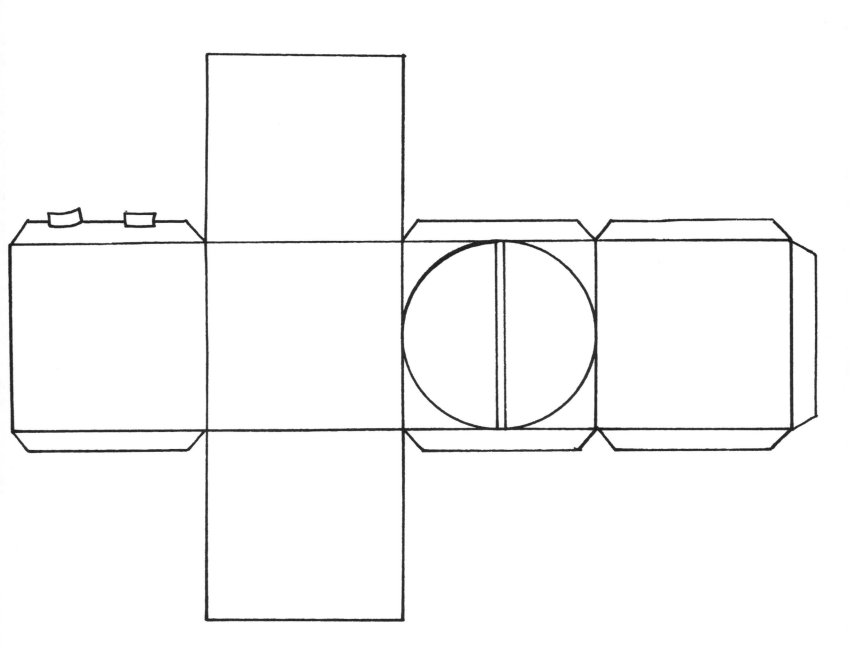

One-Point Perspective

One-point perspective is viewed when parallel lines appear to converge and disappear at one point on the horizon. If you hold the box directly in front of your eye, you will see one-point perspective. If you have ever looked down a railroad track while standing in the middle of the track, you have noticed that the tracks seem to converge at one point far in the distance and eventually disappear. This is another example of one-point perspective.

There are three different kinds of lines—vertical, horizontal, and perspective—in perspective drawing. Vertical lines run up and down. Some are straight and some run angled. Horizontal lines run from side to side like the horizon. Perspective lines converge at some point on the horizon line. One-point perspective includes all three kinds of lines.

As you draw the box, the surface that you draw on (the clear material) is called a *picture plane*. The picture plane is not limited to tracing the image through clear material; the picture plane could also be the paper you use as you draw the box.

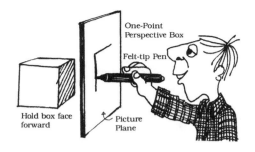

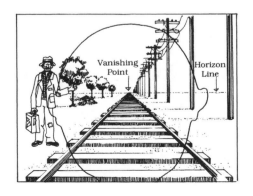

Two-Point Perspective

Two-point perspective is viewed when, from a given edge, parallel lines converge at two single points on the horizon line at opposite sides of your paper. This perspective is demonstrated by turning the box you just made so that you are looking at an edge of that box. From that edge the sides of the box seem to get smaller as they move away from the eye. The sides appear to get smaller until they vanish at two different points on the horizon line.

In the examples on the previous page and below, notice how the edges on the newspaper machine and on the cereal box appear to get smaller as they move farther away from you.

Extends toward a single Vanishing Point on the left

Extends toward a single Vanishing Point on the right

Three-Point Perspective

Three-point perspective is viewed when lines appear to converge at three given points either to the sides of the picture plane or at the top or bottom of the page, depending on where your eye level line is.

Look at the corner of the building in the following image. As the sides of the building go away from you, the two parallel edges create lines that will disappear at a point on the horizon line. As you look up at the building you will notice that the vertical lines that go up appear to get closer and

closer at the top so that they would eventually disappear at a point high above the building.

The Three Kinds of Perspective Summarized

One-Point Perspective:

- Side of box against glass
- 3 kinds of lines—vertical, horizontal, and perspective

Two-Point Perspective:

- Edge of box against glass
- 2 kinds of lines—vertical and perspective

Three-Point Perspective:

- Corner of box against glass
- 1 kind of line—perspective

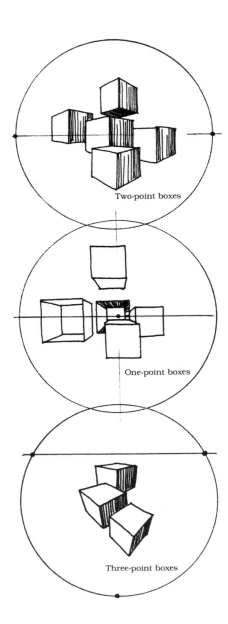

Two-point boxes

One-point boxes

Three-point boxes

Key Principles of Perspective

The key principles to remember when drawing boxes in perspective are:

1. Perspective lines converge at a vanishing point.
2. The horizon line is always horizontal.
3. The nearest angle is 90° or greater.
4. The sides of a cube are proportional to a square.

Some common errors occur when you learn to draw cubes. A few to watch for are:

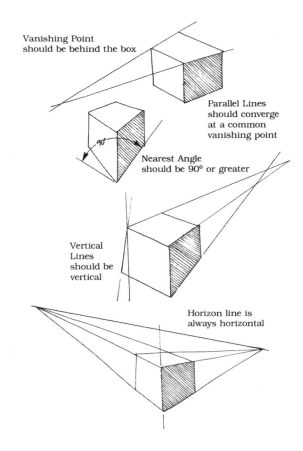

Vanishing Point should be behind the box

Parallel Lines should converge at a common vanishing point

90°

Nearest Angle should be 90° or greater

Vertical Lines should be vertical

Horizon line is always horizontal

Exercise 1.1

You need to develop a critical eye so that you can easily see if a cube is drawn in correct perspective. Here are some lines that are three sides of a square. The fourth side is missing.

You draw in the fourth line so that these squares show accurate perspective. (Hint: Slide a straight edge along until the square appears visually correct to you, and then draw the line.)

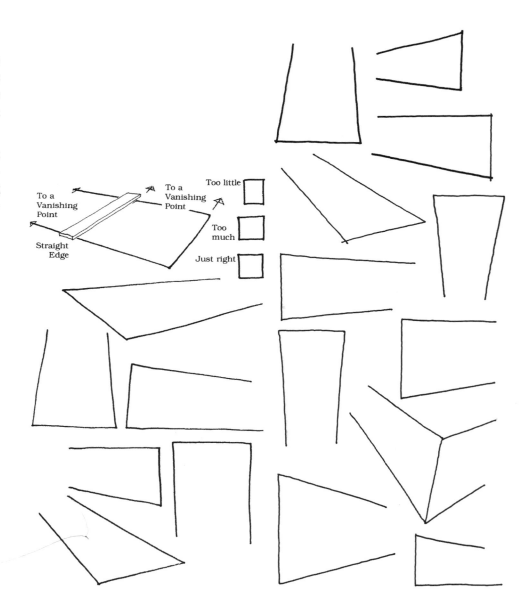

Exercise 1.2

Some of the cubes here are drawn incorrectly. Study them and identify what is wrong.

Use tracing paper to draw over the cubes so you fix what is wrong. (Hint: The cubes have one or more of these four common errors: (1) convergence, (2) horizon line, (3) nearest angle, or (4) incorrect proportion.)

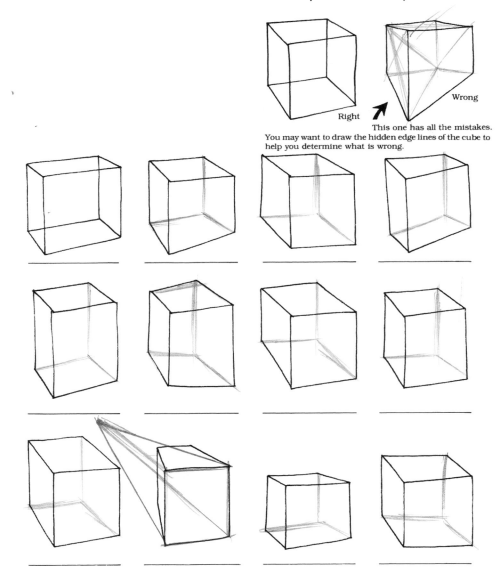

Right   Wrong

This one has all the mistakes. You may want to draw the hidden edge lines of the cube to help you determine what is wrong.

The next image depicts many different cubes within a circle with a horizon line. All of the cubes are drawn in two-point perspective. The cubes above and below the horizon line begin to distort because of the perspective drawing. Whenever you draw things in perspective, it is helpful to imagine that you are drawing within the limits of a circle. If you draw beyond that imaginary circle, then the cubes begin to appear so distorted that they won't seem real.

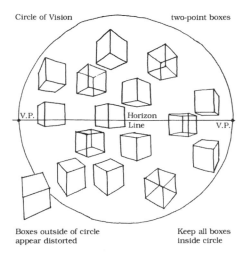

Drawing One-Point Boxes

You have three kinds of lines in one-point perspective—vertical lines, horizontal lines, and perspective lines. If you seem to have trouble drawing things correctly, draw the box as though it were transparent so that you can see the hidden sides, edges, and corners. Then erase the hidden lines, once you have everything drawn correctly, thus leaving a solid box.

In one-point perspective, the farther away from the central vanishing point, the closer to the outer edge to the circle, the more distortion. This distortion that occurs when you near the outer limits of the circle is more pronounced with one-point perspective than with two- and three-point perspective.

Drawing Two-Point Boxes

Drawing in two-point perspective is the easiest of all perspective drawing for most people. You have only two kinds of lines—perspective lines or vertical lines. If you have trouble drawing things correctly, draw the box as though it were transparent so that you can see the hidden sides, edges, and corners. Then erase the hidden lines after you have drawn everything correctly.

Drawing Three-Point Boxes

There is only one kind of line in three-point perspective—perspective lines. If you have difficulty drawing three-point perspective boxes correctly, draw the box as though it were transparent so that you can see the hidden sides, edges, and corners. After you have everything drawn correctly, erase the hidden lines.

The boxes inside the following circle look like you are looking down on them. To reverse the point of view, simply turn this book upside down. The boxes will then look like you are beneath them.

Exercise 1.3

Using the following circle, do the following:

- Draw 2 more boxes anywhere within the circle.
- Draw 2 boxes that sit in front of or behind other boxes.
- When finished, there will be 5 boxes total inside the circle.

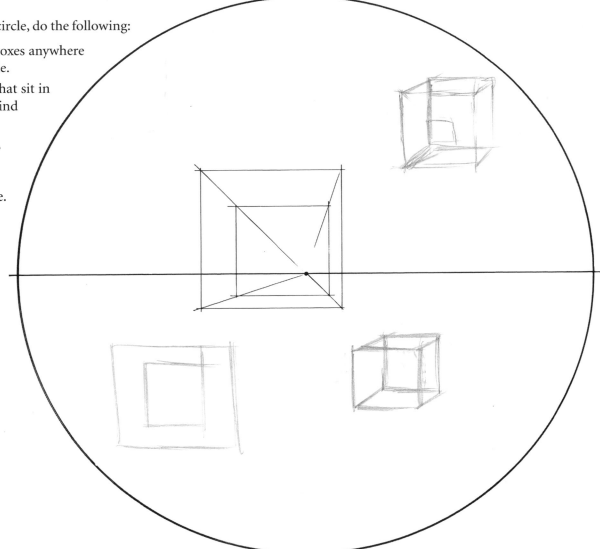

Exercise 1.4

Study the box in the following circle, and then do the following:

- Finish drawing the other box that is started in the lower half of the circle.

- Draw 3 more boxes any-where within the circle.

- Draw 2 boxes that sit in front of or behind other boxes.

- When finished, there will be 7 boxes total inside the circle.

Here is a hint to use when drawing objects. The outside lines of the object should be drawn darker and heavier. The darker out-side edges make each object appear to stand by itself either in front of or behind another object.

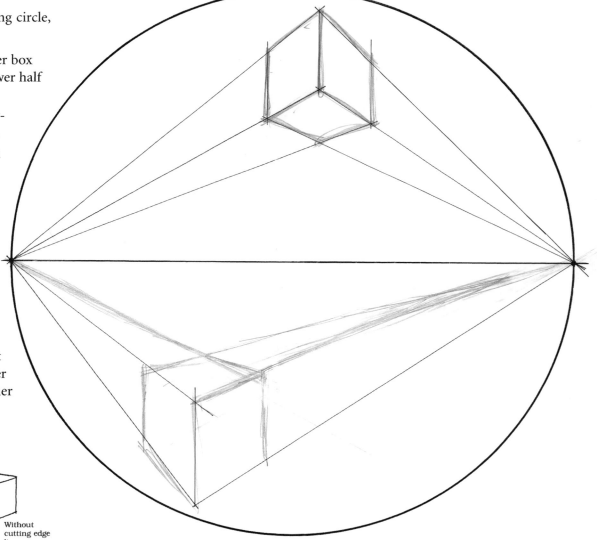

Cutting edge lines   Without cutting edge lines

Exercise 1.5

Study the box in the following circle, and then do the following:

- Draw 3 more boxes anywhere within the circle.
- Draw 2 boxes that sit in front of or behind other boxes.
- When finished, there will be 6 boxes total inside the circle.

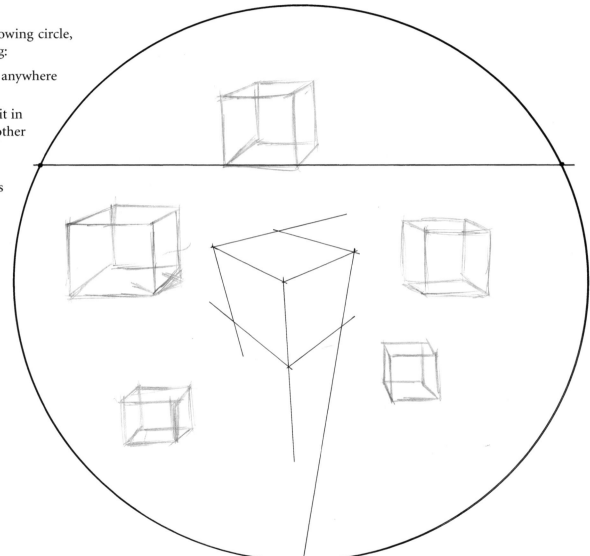

Dividing a Square

As shown in the following example, diagonal lines drawn from corner to corner of a square cross in the exact middle of that square. A line drawn from the middle of the square to the vanishing point bisects the edge at midpoint. If you draw a line from the corner through the midpoint of the side, this line will cross the bottom line of the square giving you the location of the far corner of the next square. This principle is used to help divide a square into equal segments or to enlarge a square in equal segments.

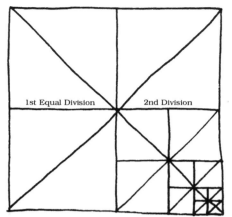

1st Equal Division   2nd Division

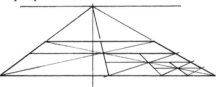

Below is a square drawn in perspective. You are above the square looking down on it. Using the diagonal to divide the square applies in perspective also.

The lower half of the next example demonstrates a square drawn in perspective. In this drawing, you are above the square looking down on it. As you can see in the example, the diagonal method of dividing a square applies in perspective drawing as well.

Exercise 1.6

In the following examples, draw diagonals to cut the squares and cubes directly in half. Begin by dividing them in half, and then divide one side into quarters. You will need to draw the hidden edges (sides of cubes away from you that you don't see) of the cubes in order to know where to divide them.

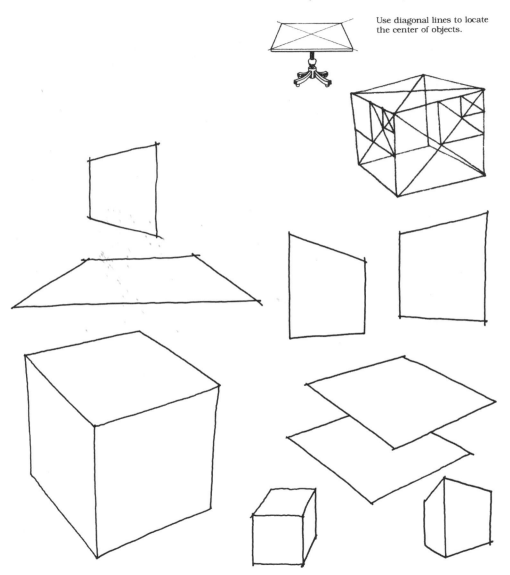

Use diagonal lines to locate the center of objects.

Units of Measurement

A cube can act as a standard of measurement. The cubes shown here are all the same size, but they appear to be different sizes because of the surroundings—the woman, the tiny person, the man, the shoe. These different cubes can represent different units of measurement such as one inch, one foot, one mile, and so on depending on the surroundings that create scale.

The following box is divided into equal units. The box measures 10 units tall × 5 units wide × 10 units deep. If the units were not specified, you could still determine the proportion because the box is half as wide as it is tall.

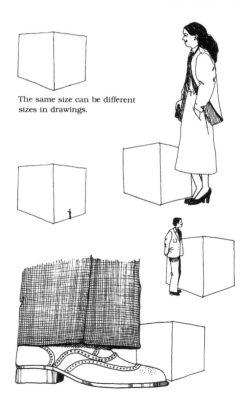

The same size can be different sizes in drawings.

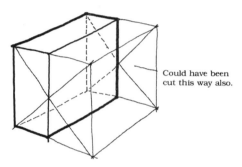

Could have been cut this way also.

Exercise 1.7

Using the following cubes, determine the proportions and divide them accordingly. Use cubes as units of measurement. Divide the cubes to get correct proportions. The same size cube can represent different units of measurement.

Draw this cube as 5 × 5 × 10.

Draw this cube as 10 × 10 × 5.

Draw this cube as 1 × 1 × 0.5.

Draw this cube as 1 × 2 × 3.

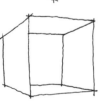

Draw this cube as 2 × 1.5 × 1.

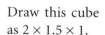

Draw this cube as 100 × 100 × 75.

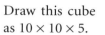
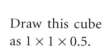

Adding Squares

The same principle of using diagonal lines to find the exact middle of the sides of a box also enables you to draw more than one square in perspective. Begin by finding the exact middle of the square, and then extend a line from the corner through the middle of the far side. Where that line intersects, the bottom perspective line shows you the length of the next square in perspective, as shown in the following example.

Squares drawn in perspective appear to diminish in size. You can find the correct rate that they diminish by drawing the diagonal lines to find the center of the far edge of the square. Draw another diagonal line from the corner of the square directly through the midpoint of the edge and down to where it finds the bottom corner of the next square.

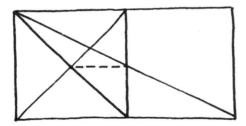

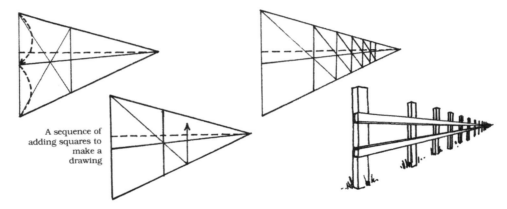

A sequence of adding squares to make a drawing

Exercise 1.8

Use this technique to determine where the next square in succession should be located based on the following square, which is drawn in perspective.

Add as many squares as you can to the following drawings.

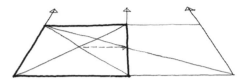

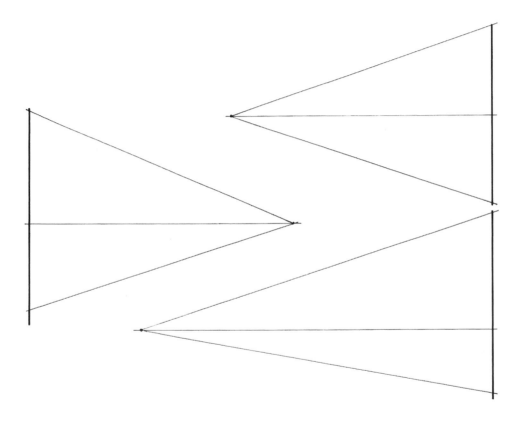

Multiplying Squares

These squares drawn in perspective easily can become cubes. The same principles that apply to the square apply to the cube or box. Just stack cubes on top of one another or next to one another to draw larger, more complicated objects.

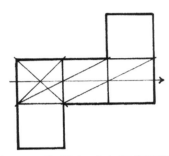

The same method that works in two dimensions will also work in three dimensions.

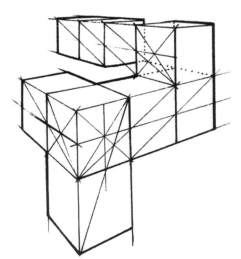

To draw other squares, cubes, or boxes in correct proportion, first use the diagonal to find the center of the side. Draw a line from the center of the side to the vanishing point—this bisects the far side exactly in half. Draw a line from the corner through the center of the far side to where it intersects with the bottom perspective line of the box. This intersection between the diagonal through the side to the bottom gives you the size of the next square or box in succession.

Exercise 1.9

Use tracing paper to draw the cube shown here. Draw 3 cubes in every direction—in front, behind, above, below, to the right, and to the left—from the original cube.

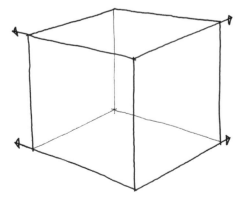

Another principle that you will find useful when multiplying squares is that diagonal lines converge at a single vanishing point. The following illustration demonstrates how this works. The boxes must be equal in size (squares in this example), and the sides of the box must be parallel.

You can apply this principle to draw objects in perspective. If you can determine diagonal lines of boxes, you can then find the far corner and can add more boxes quickly. The following cube is taken from the previous example of many cubes drawn in

perspective. As shown here, it becomes easy to add more cubes to this one because the diagonal lines converge at a vanishing point making it easy to determine where the corners of the additional cubes will be located.

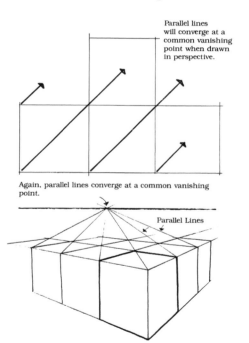

Parallel lines will converge at a common vanishing point when drawn in perspective.

Again, parallel lines converge at a common vanishing point.

Parallel Lines

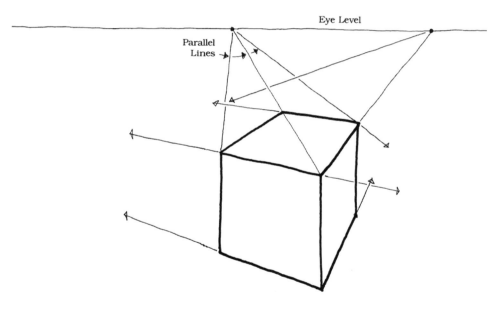

Eye Level

Parallel Lines

Exercise 1.10

Use tracing paper to draw cubes in both directions—one to the right and two to the left—of the cube shown here.

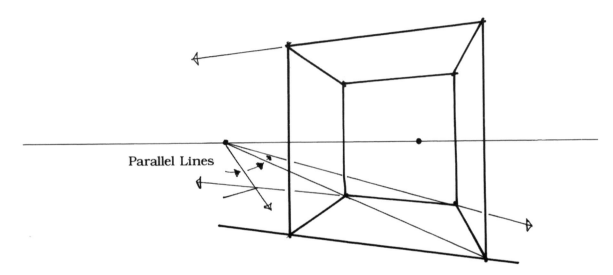

Parallel Lines

Adding Boxes Vertically

Parallel lines (sides of a flat surface that sets at an angle such as a roof top or open box lid) converge at a single point. You could use this knowledge to help you draw the rooftop of a building. The lines that form the side of that roof, when extended, converge at a vanishing point directly above the vanishing point on the horizon line. This point above the horizon line is called a *trace*. You will find it useful to know that these lines do converge at a point above or below the vanishing point on the horizon line.

Exercise 1.11

Use tracing paper to add two cubes in every direction from the cube shown here. Add 2 cubes above, 2 below, 2 behind, 2 in front of, and 2 on each side of the original box.

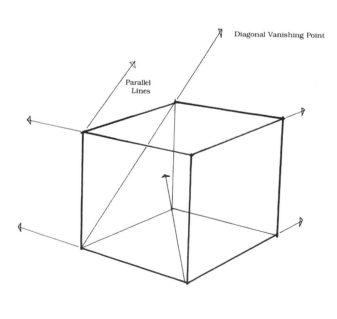

To the Vanishing Point

House

Opened Box

The perspective edge lines of a slanted surface—such as an open lid on a box or a roof—go to a vanishing point above or below the vanishing point on the horizon line.

Diagonal Vanishing Point

Parallel Lines

To V.P.

To the Vanishing Point

V.P.

Diagonal Vanishing Point

Parallel Lines

Assorted Boxes

So far we have concentrated on cubes—boxes with equally sized sides. However, you also need to be able to draw different sized boxes. You can create odd sized boxes by butting two or more cubes together, as shown in the following examples of assorted box sizes.

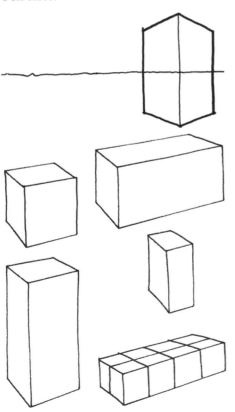

Exercise 1.12

Practice applying the principles you've learned by creating odd sized boxes. Strive to draw accurate perspective without having to draw all of the hidden sides, vanishing points, and converging lines. You should become so familiar with how things should look when drawn correctly that you can do it right the first time.

- Draw a 1 × 2 × 1 box using two-point perspective at eye level.

- Draw a 2.5 × 2 × 3 box using two-point perspective below eye level.

- Draw a 2 × 4 × 1 box using one-point perspective below eye level.

- Draw a 2 × 2 × 5 box with an open top so that you can see inside using one-point perspective at eye level.

- Draw a 5 × 5 × 10 box using one-point perspective below eye level so that you are looking inside.

- Draw a 5 × 7 × 9 box using three-point perspective at eye level.

- Draw a 6.5 × 5 × 3 box using three-point perspective at eye level.

- Choose 2 or more boxes that you want to draw. Decide the eye level and the perspective that you want to see and draw them.

Different Views

Now that you have learned how to draw boxes and squares, you can take it to the next level by using those boxes to create different images. When drawing buildings for architecture, you show different views of the proposed building—front view, side view, and top view. These views are as if you placed your building within a glass box and then traced the appropriate view. If you look down, directly on top of your box, you see the top view of the building. If you look at one side, you see the side view, and so on.

You need to learn how to convert those three different views into a three-dimensional object. Remember that these different views are as though you were peeling away the sides of a box with an object drawn on the sides of that box. They are flat views of a three-dimensional object.

Place the object inside a transparent box. The views are drawn on the sides of the box, and then the box is unfolded.

When it is completely unfolded, you see the different views of the object.

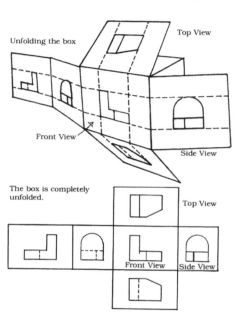

Unfolding the box
Top View
Front View
Side View

The box is completely unfolded.
Top View
Front View   Side View

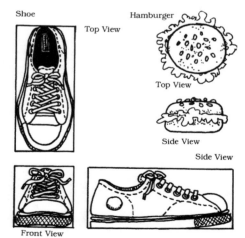

Shoe
Top View
Front View

Hamburger
Top View
Side View
Side View

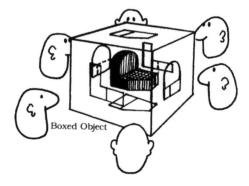

Boxed Object

Exercise 1.13

Draw the top, front, and side views of the table below.

Draw the views of the object shown here.

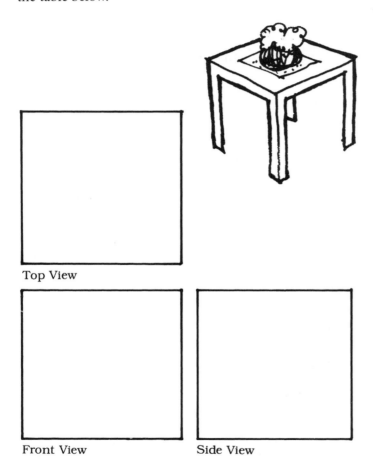

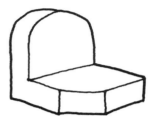

Top View

Front View

Side View

Top

Front

Side

Visualizing the Object

This section contains the top, front, and side views of many different objects. You need to learn how to visualize those objects as they really look. In other words, you need to recognize the three-dimensional object by seeing the two-dimensional top, front, and side views.

Exercise 1.14

Use additional sheets of paper to draw the three-dimensional view of the following objects based on the two-dimension drawings, as shown for the first object. (Hint: Hidden lines are indicated by a dashed line. These dashed lines are edges that you cannot see from the view that you are looking at. The dashed lines are as if you were looking at the object with x-ray vision so that you could see the hidden edges.)

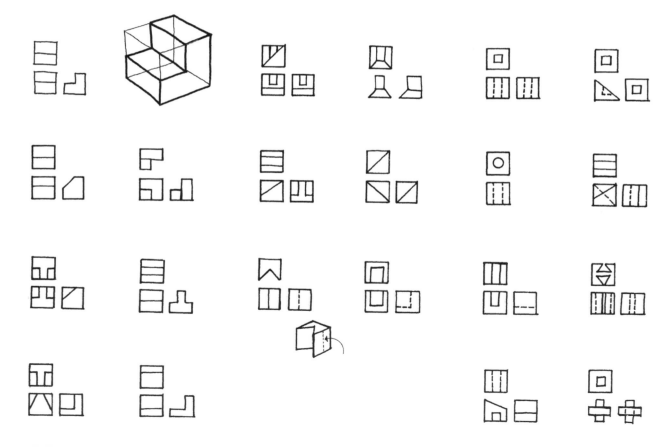

Complicated Objects

You can draw complex and complicated objects by using more than one box to help you.

Exercise 1.15

Use additional sheets of paper to draw the three-dimensional view of the objects shown here.

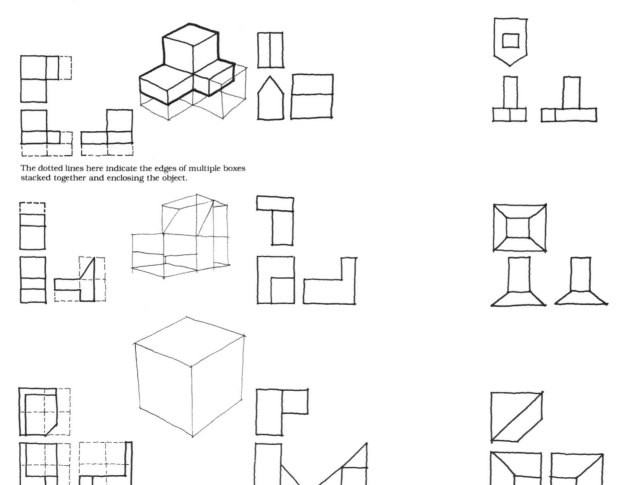

The dotted lines here indicate the edges of multiple boxes stacked together and enclosing the object.

Drawing Cube Shelving

Abstracta is a method of using tubing that connects at the corners to form boxes. When stacked in different configurations, these boxes form shelving for display.

Exercise 1.16

Use tracing paper to evolve the following drawing to include at least 7 more cubes of shelves that create your own abstracta display case.

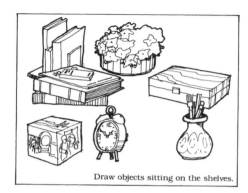

This shelving is just a series of boxes.

Recreate these objects sitting on the shelves of your display case.

Draw objects sitting on the shelves.

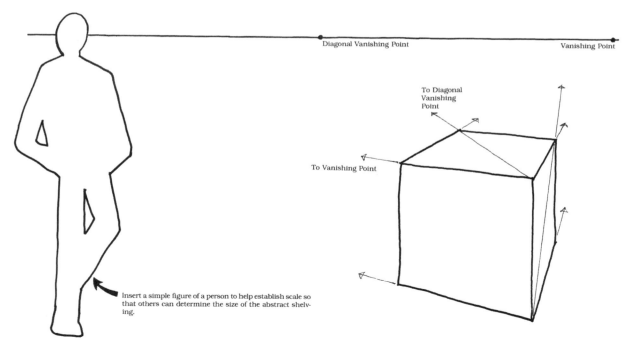

Diagonal Vanishing Point

Vanishing Point

To Diagonal Vanishing Point

To Vanishing Point

Insert a simple figure of a person to help establish scale so that others can determine the size of the abstract shelving.

Drawing a Chair

If you can draw a cube, then you can apply the cube method to draw other objects. For example, I created a chair by beginning first with a cube and then erasing the lines of the cube so that all that remains is the chair.

Exercise 1.17

Draw 5 chairs using the cube technique. Begin by completing the 2 drawings started in the following example, and then create 3 of your own from scratch.

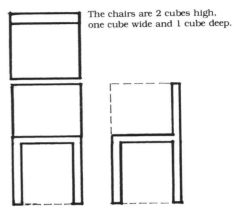

The chairs are 2 cubes high, one cube wide and 1 cube deep.

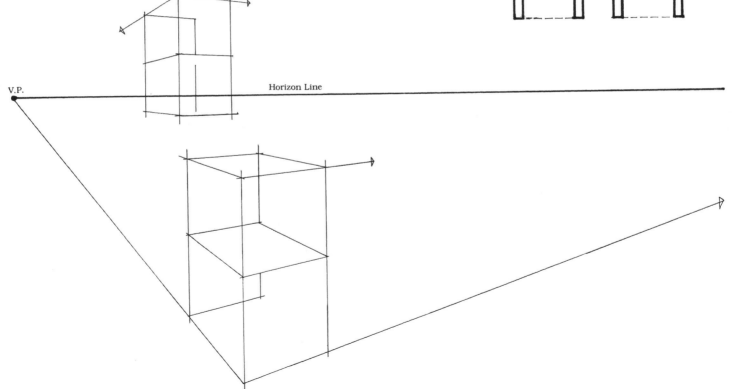

The chairs shown here look different from one another, but they were all made using the same cube technique. Take a look around you or in magazines for inspiration and draw at least 3 different chair styles.

Drawing a Sofa

You also can draw a sofa using the cube method. A sofa is essentially an extended chair, so you can draw a sofa by simply stacking three or four chairs next to one another.

Exercise 1.18

Draw 2 different sofas using the same principle of different cubes stacked next each other.

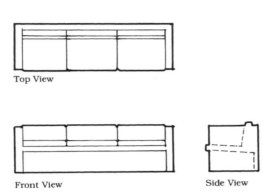

Top View

Front View

Side View

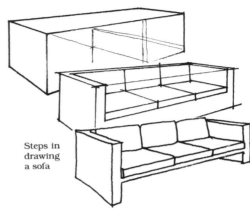

Steps in drawing a sofa

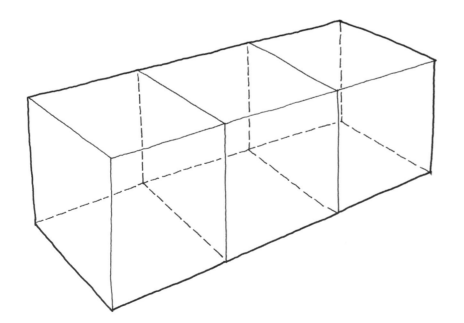

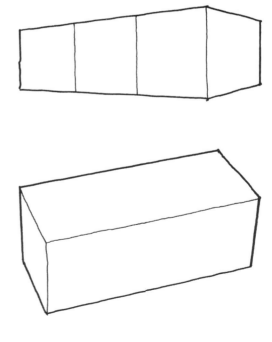

Drawing Other Objects

The following objects—swimming pool, refrigerator, office building, and vending machine—were drawn using the box method.

Exercise 1.19

Use the box method to draw the objects identified. I have provided the box; you finish the object to create a finished drawing.

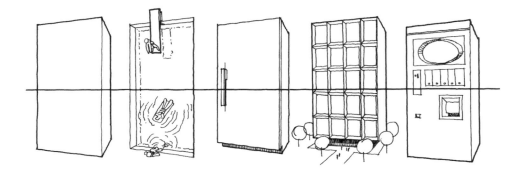

■ A box of tissue

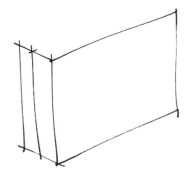

■ A suitcase

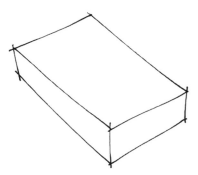

■ A bed

■ A car

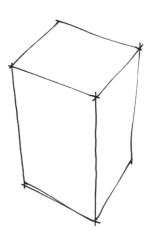

■ A tall building with a helicopter landing pad on the roof

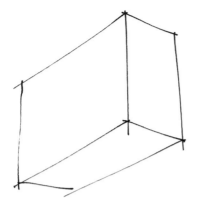

▪ An upside-down suitcase

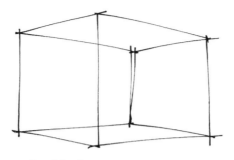

▪ Bunkbeds

▪ A skyscraper

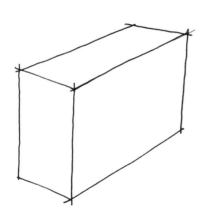

▪ A television

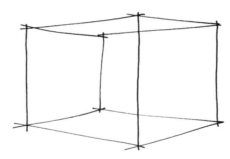

▪ A table

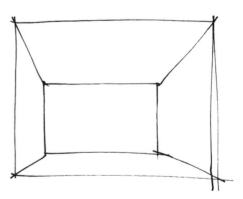

▪ A children's bedroom schematic

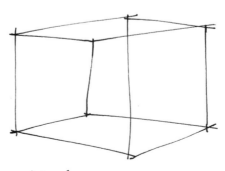

▪ A trunk

Drawing a Building

Drawing the exterior of a building is accomplished by using the same principle as drawing previous objects. You stack different squares or cubes next to one another to form a basic building. Use the principles of diagonal lines to find how to correctly stack your cubes in perspective. Then create the different angles, views, and surfaces for the building.

The following example is a building I constructed using cubes to help draw the final view of that building. It was done simply by extending cubes. We started with one cube and then extended cubes in different directions to get the other sides and surfaces of the building.

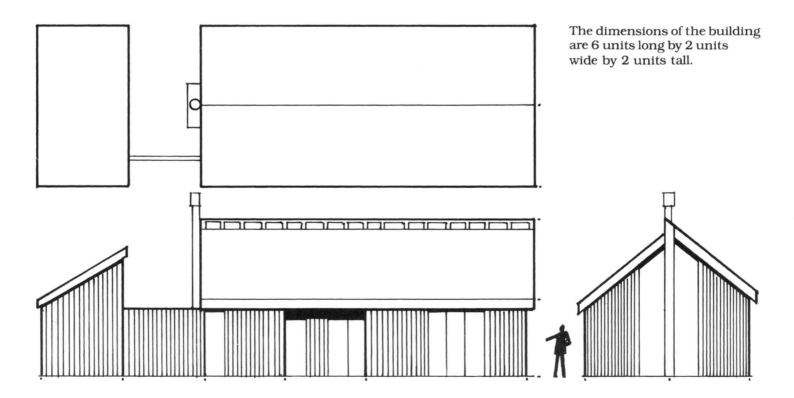

The dimensions of the building are 6 units long by 2 units wide by 2 units tall.

Exercise 1.20

Place a piece of tracing paper over the building shown here to trace the drawing, and then finish it by adding windows, doors, landscaping, or whatever you imagine.

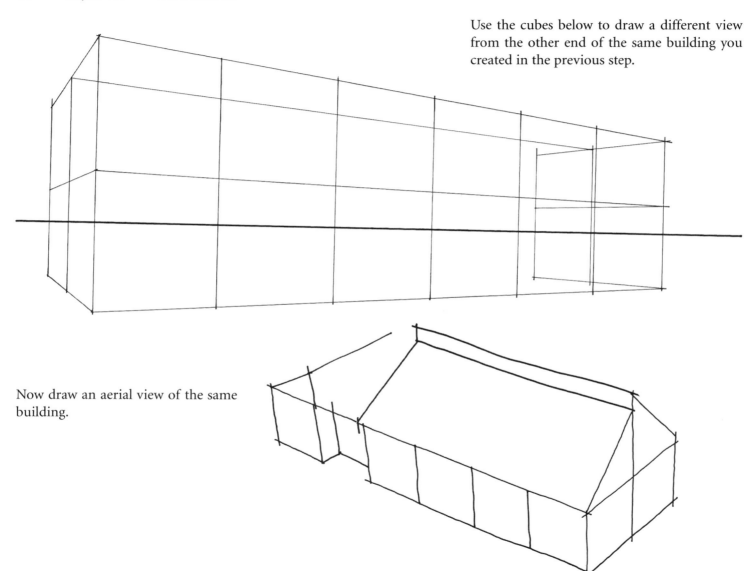

Use the cubes below to draw a different view from the other end of the same building you created in the previous step.

Now draw an aerial view of the same building.

Drawing Interiors

In architecture and interior design you need to learn how to draw objects within a room. Drawing objects within a room starts with a floor plan (a top view of the room). It is very simple. Use boxes and cubes to create different furniture or objects for the room, and then use the top view to place everything in the room.

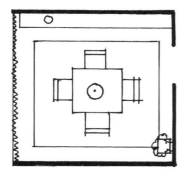

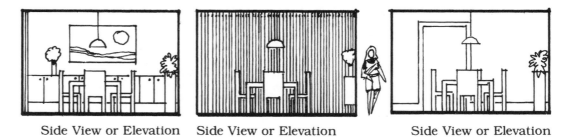

Side View or Elevation   Side View or Elevation   Side View or Elevation

The dimensions of the room are 12 x 12 x 8.

Top View or Plan View

The following steps were used to create the interior of the room shown here. Study each step until you understand exactly what has been done. The whole process looks complicated, but it isn't. The process looks time consuming, but it isn't when compared to other drawing methods. It took only a few minutes to draw what is shown here. These are my thumbnail sketches of the interior shown full-size on the following page.

Draw a square; it is 12 feet square

Find the midpoint of the side

Divide the side into equal units—6 below the midpoint

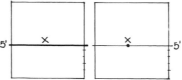

Find eye level—usually the 5 foot mark

Draw the horizon line and vanishing point

Draw the perspective lines

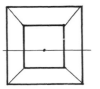

Estimate the depth of your 12 x 12 x 8 room.

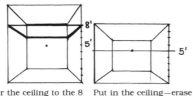

Lower the ceiling to the 8 foot mark

Put in the ceiling—erase the excess

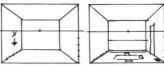

Put in marks for depth measurement—use the diagonals to find the midpoint

Draw views on the outside surfaces

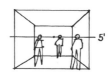

Put in human figures to establish scale

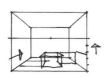

Project views to draw objects

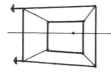

The room can be made more interesting in 2-point perspective

Remember the basic principles in dealing with boxes. In most complex drawings they are just repeated over and over again.

Exercise 1.21

Place tracing paper over the following drawing. Finish and refine the room by adding paintings on the walls, include lamps, refine the roughed in furniture, add windows, whatever you envision.

Now draw another point of view of the same room by looking in from one of the other walls.

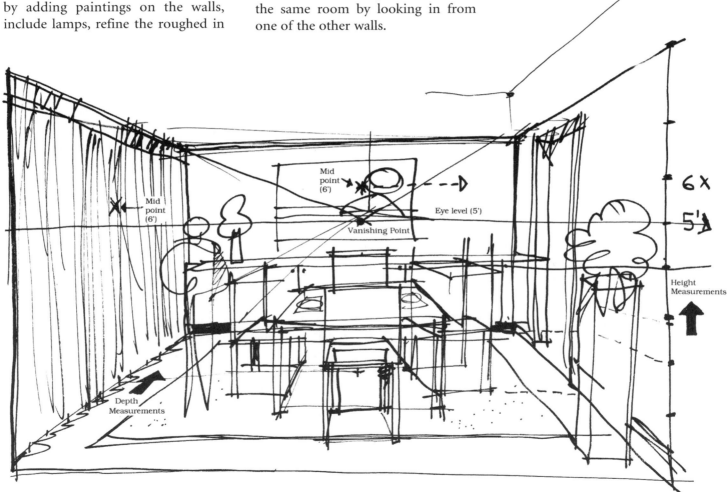

Drawing Basic Shapes

All objects are made up from four basic shapes—cube, sphere, cylinder, or cone. You can use the box method to accurately draw these shapes to round out your body of knowledge of all basic shapes needed to create accurate drawings. If you learn to see objects as basic shapes, you will more easily be able to draw the objects.

At least once in your drawing experiences you will encounter an instance when your drawing "just doesn't look right." When this occurs, go back to the basics. First, construct your drawing using basic shapes—cubes, spheres, cylinders, and cones—to give form to the objects. Then evolve these basic shapes until you create the drawing that you want.

Circles and Ellipses

Drawing an accurate circle can be a bit more difficult that it sounds, but it can be done with practice. To draw a perfect circle, first draw a square and then draw a circle inside the square. Draw diagonal lines from the midpoint of the sides of the square. Plot a point 1/3 in from the corner on the diagonal. Now draw a gentle curve that passes through the points 1/3 in on the diagonals and touches all four midpoints of the sides of the square.

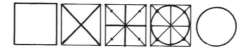

Take a coin or some other perfectly round object and hold it level with your eye. If you look straight on that object, you will see that it is exactly flat—a straight line. As you look at the object above or below eye level you see different views of it, including elongated circles, which are *ellipses* or circles viewed in perspective.

Circular objects that you see in real life—tires, cups, coins, saucers, discs, and so on—appear as an ellipse because you see them in perspective most of the time.

Drawing an ellipse is a simple process. Begin by drawing a perfect circle using the previous technique, except draw the square in perspective this time. When drawn in perspective, the circle in the square is an ellipse.

Exercise 1.22

Get the cube that you previously cut out of this book and assembled to study perspective. The cube has a circle drawn on one of the sides. Cut out that circle and draw two perpendicular lines to form an X through the center point of the circle. Push a straight pin through the center of the circle, and hold the pin between your fingers. Rotate your circle to the different positions as shown in the following example. Observe what happens to the circle and the lines. As you move the circle, one line appears to shorten—this is the minor axis. The other line is longer—the major axis.

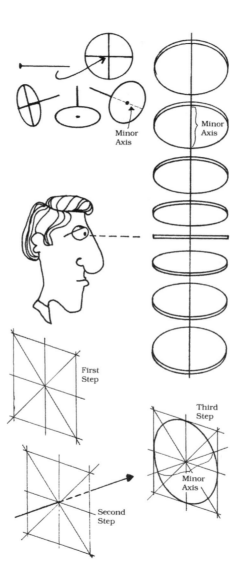

Minor Axis

Minor Axis

First Step

Second Step

Third Step

Minor Axis

Note: The minor axis is the narrowest diameter of an ellipse. The minor axis line always lines up with the pin that you have put through the center of the circle as in the example shown here. It also is the direction of an axle on a wheel or the shaft on a cylinder or the center of a cone. Keep this in mind to eliminate a lot of distortion problems.

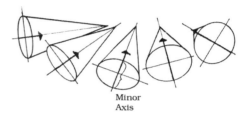

Minor Axis

Draw a page of squares in perspective and draw ellipses in them.

Spheres

Many people think that drawing a sphere is the same as drawing a circle. That is not exactly correct. A circle is two dimensional while a sphere is three dimensional, as shown in the following example.

To draw an accurate sphere, begin by drawing a cube. Then draw two dissecting planes that cut the cube in half both vertically and horizontally. Draw ellipses within the planes in the square. Touch the mid-points of the squares within the cube.

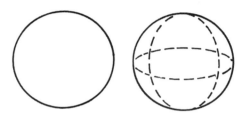

Exercise 1.23

The following sphere demonstrates what it would look like if 1/4 of the sphere were cut away. Draw a different point of view than shown here.

Draw the sphere with 1/2 cut away as shown here. Again, draw a different point of view than shown in the example.

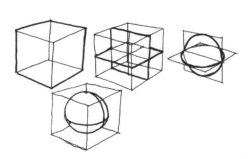

Cylinders and Cones

To draw a cylinder, begin by drawing a box in perspective. Then draw ellipses on opposite sides of the box. Connect these circles with straight lines to form a cylinder as in the following illustration.

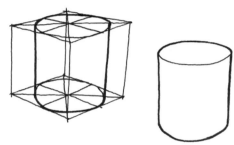

Drawing a cone is similar to drawing a cylinder, except this time draw an ellipse on only one side of the box. Find the midpoint on the opposite side of the box, and draw lines from the midpoint to the edges of the circle. You now have a cone as shown here.

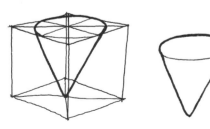

Exercise 1.24

The following are examples of objects drawn using basic shapes. Complete each drawing as indicated.

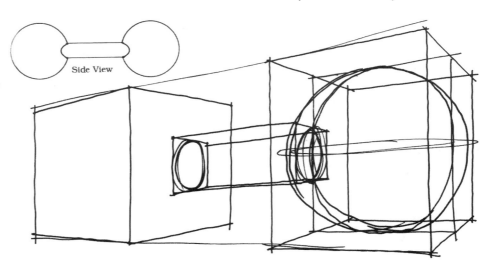

Side View

Side View

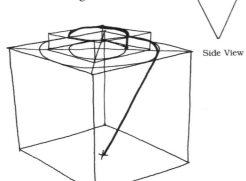

Complete the object that is partially drawn in below.

Side View

Side View

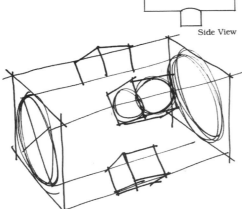

Create perspective drawings for the objects shown here.

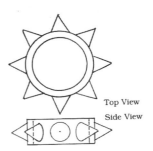

Top View

Side View

Exercise 1.25

Re-create a three-dimensional view of the following objects shown in the two-dimensional drawings. This is a bit more difficult than the similar exercise you completed earlier in this chapter because this time the objects have circles or circular shapes in them.

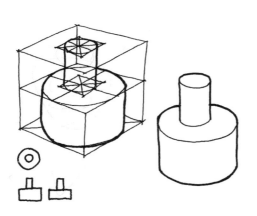

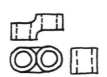

Exercise 1.26

Draw the following objects:

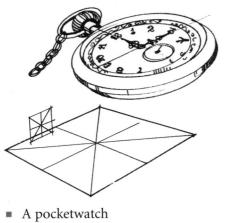

■ A pocketwatch

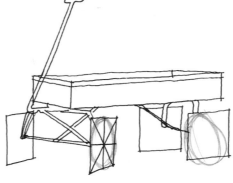

■ A wagon

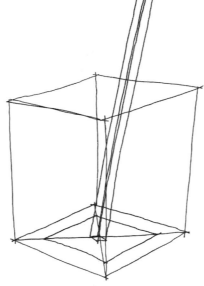

■ A drinking glass with a straw in it

■ A planter

Exercise 1.27

The following unfinished sketch has many circular shapes. Most of these circular shapes appear as ellipses because they are circles drawn in perspective. The wheels and tires are examples.

Using tracing paper refine the following incomplete drawing until you evolve a drawing of a three-wheel car that you envision.

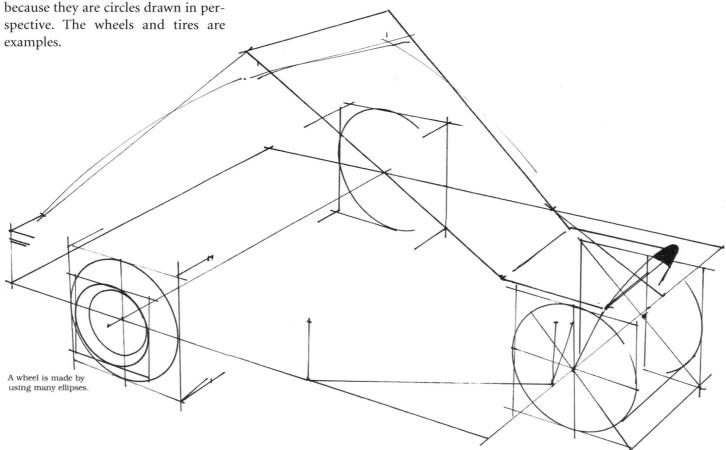

A wheel is made by using many ellipses.

Exercise 1.28

The machine shown here converts spheres into cubes. The machine starts with spheres (small balls) and it gradually changes them into cubes through seven different steps.

Create your own machine that changes one basic shape into another. In drawing your machine, use all of the basic shapes for the various parts of the machine. Your machine should use seven steps to convert one basic shape into the other. You'll know that your machine is correctly drawn if someone else can accurately identify the conversion process that you have attempted to illustrate.

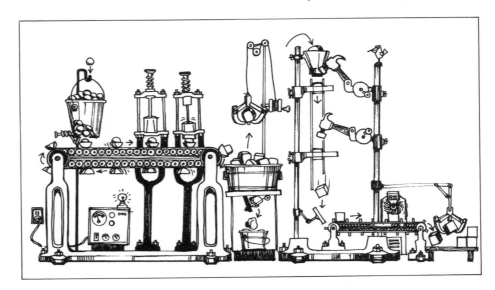

Exercise 1.29

Draw a bird's eye view of where you are now. Use basic shapes to draw the different forms as shown in the following example. Label all of the streets, buildings, and rooms shown in your drawing.

Exercise 1.30

Combine different basic shapes to create a half-insect, half-machine being. You may need to refer to photos of heavy machinery or various insects to get ideas for your new creation.

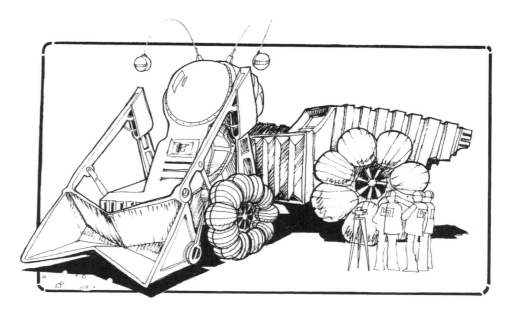

Exercise 1.31

The following image is a light made up of a series of cones.

- Draw a piece of furniture or an appliance using all the basic shapes—a sphere, cylinder, cube, and cone. (Your designs will probably be more fantasy than reality, which is fine for this exercise.)

- Draw a toaster from a cone, a cube, and 2 spheres.

- Draw a radio from 2 spheres and a cylinder.

- Draw a chair from 2 spheres and a cube.

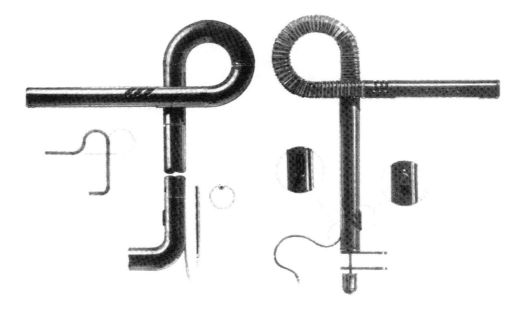

The Grid Method

The grid method is a way of enlarging, reducing, or putting in perspective any object that you draw. Place a grid over your drawing, and then make a new grid apart from your drawing. To finish, transfer your drawing square by square from the old grid to the new one.

To apply the grid method to a drawing, take your original object and place a grid system of equal size squares on top of it. Make a new grid and transfer your drawing one square at a time.

You can enlarge or reduce the object by using the grid. If you want the copy to be larger than the original, use larger squares for the new grid and copy what you see in the original square-by-square. Because the second grid is larger, the finished copy will be larger than the original. In a like manner, you can reduce something by using smaller squares than in the original grid.

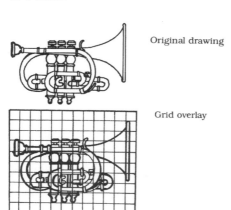

Original drawing

Grid overlay

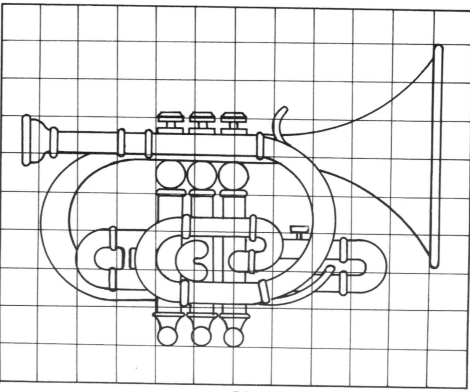

Enlarged grid with drawing in place

If you want to draw an object in perspective, the grid that you transfer onto should be drawn in perspective. The following illustration shows how it's done.

Grid drawn in perspective with drawing in place

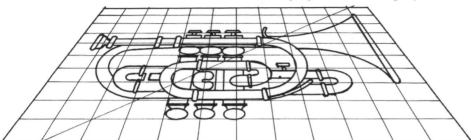

Drawing Buildings and Landscapes

You will find the grid method helpful when drawing buildings and landscapes. By superimposing a grid over views of a building or landscape, you can transfer the image easily onto a new surface.

Begin by placing a grid over the original drawing. Lay a piece of tracing paper over a new grid, and transfer the old drawing one square at a time. Because you are drawing on tracing paper with the new grid underneath, your final drawing will not have a visible grid. The drawing will be accurate because the grid method was used, but it will not be apparent in the final drawing.

Exercise 1.32

Place tracing paper over the following grid and transfer the small views of the park structure onto it in a perspective drawing. (Hint: Before transferring the views to the perspective drawing, draw a grid of equal squares over the small views of the park.)

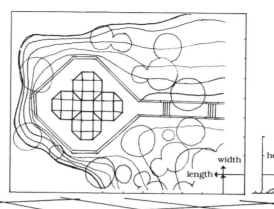

width

height

length

Contour Lines

Contour lines are lines that wrap around objects to depict what the surface of the object is like. Contour lines make two-dimensional flat objects appear to be solid, whole objects.

The following example shows an oval object before and after adding contour lines. As you can see the addition of the contour lines adds dimension to the object to make it more recognizable.

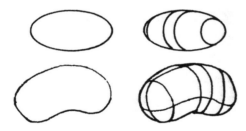

When adding contour lines to your drawings you should become conscious of your hand holding the pen and its pressure on the paper. Don't just draw the lines over the shape; feel the shape. Whether it is a car or a face, use your eye and hand to feel the contour line as it caresses the surface. Sense the contour as it travels down, around, and into the object exerting pressure on the paper as needed. With contour lines more than any other technique, you must respond to that two-dimensional drawing as an actual three-dimensional object.

I had one student who aspired to design automobiles. Before coming to my class, he was frustrated with the automobile drawings he created. Once we began drawing contour lines, he easily understood what was lacking from his earlier drawings. The addition of proper contour lines gave his drawings that three-dimensional feeling that he and the viewer needed in order to *feel* the car.

No matter what the object—a car, piece of furniture, topographical map, whatever—contour lines provide a clear understanding of the dimension of the object in your drawing.

Architectural renderings of buildings and sites often use contour lines to provide a three-dimensional understanding of the building. The building illustrations shown here are enhanced by contour lines. Without the lines, the drawings would appear rather dull and non-descript. The contour lines give form to the buildings.

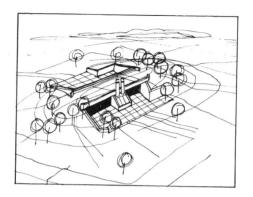

Exercise 1.33

Using the following drawing as an example, draw the contour lines around tree trunks. Feel the surface as you do it. Know exactly where the bark goes in and out, where the knots are, where the imperfections in wood appear. Those contour lines will help you understand the three-dimensional aspects of the wood.

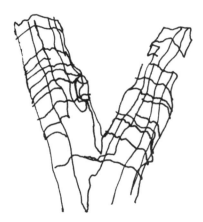

Exercise 1.34

Add contour lines to the objects on the next page. Feel the form as you draw each object. Vary the pressure of your pen, and be sure to put a dark outer line—a cutting edge line—around each object.

Exercise 1.35

Use contour lines to create a speed shape. A speed shape can be something like the automobile shown here, or a speed boat, race car, rocket, airplane, or any other object that moves fast.

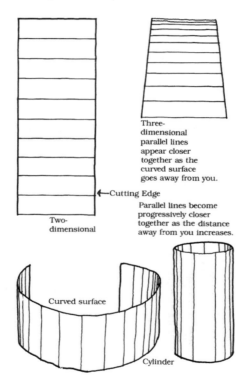

Exercise 1.36

As parallel lines move away from you, they appear to get closer and closer to each other. The ties on railroad tracks are an example of this visual phenomenon. The ties appear to get closer together as the tracks get farther away from you.

The following illustration demonstrates what happens to parallel lines when drawn in perspective. Also, lines that curve around a surface appear to get closer as the surface curves away from you, as shown in the following examples.

Three-dimensional parallel lines appear closer together as the curved surface goes away from you.

←Cutting Edge

Parallel lines become progressively closer together as the distance away from you increases.

Two-dimensional

Curved surface

Cylinder

Draw equally distant lines on the objects shown here. Remember that even though the lines are equidistant, they appear to get closer or farther apart as the surface weaves back and forth or goes into the distance.

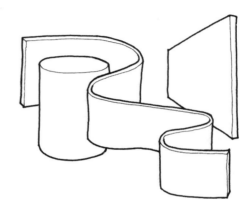

Exercise 1.37

Contour lines can change the entire appearance of an object. The car shown in the following example is a new design created by adding new contour lines to an existing vehicle to change the door lines, the molding down the side of the car, and the fender shapes. These changes have modified the entire appearance of the vehicle.

Select several photos of existing cars or trucks, and use tracing paper to add new contour lines to change the appearance of each vehicle.

Shading

We see everything in life because a light source reflects off the surface. These reflections off objects are never pure, solid tones. They are varying degrees of light or dark, which is known as *shading*.

Shading gives form to objects. The basic shapes shown here demonstrate different shading techniques. The principle behind the shading process is quite simple: The closer to the direct light source, the lighter the tone of the object. (And, conversely, the farther from the light source, the darker the tone of the object.)

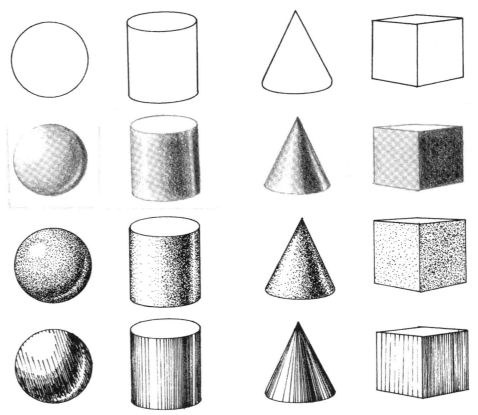

Many degrees of shading values can be seen on any object in real life. To make things more simple for Rapid Viz drawing, I suggest that you limit all objects to having only four degrees of value—light, light gray, dark gray, and black.

Light   Light Gray   Dark Gray   Black

The following cube demonstrates the four different degrees of value for shading. Speed is important when shading. Don't waste time trying to create the perfect shading value. Work quickly using the four values listed previously.

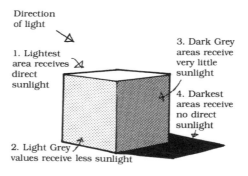

Direction of light

1. Lightest area receives direct sunlight

2. Light Grey values receive less sunlight

3. Dark Grey areas receive very little sunlight

4. Darkest areas receive no direct sunlight

Remember that the direction of the light source determines the value of the shading on the surface of the object.

Before you begin the shading exercises, experiment with your drawing tool (pen or pencil) and the drawing surface (paper). Some types of paper soak up pen ink, while others don't. Pen ink or pencil lead that looks gray on one type of paper may look jet black on another. Get the feel of the tool and the paper before you begin any drawing.

Exercise 1.38

Use a felt tip pen or a pencil to shade the following box using one of the four values.

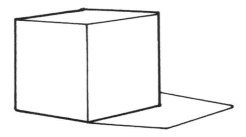

Exercise 1.39

Apply shading to the object shown here. The areas have been marked to indicate which shading value they should be (1 is the lightest, and 4 is the darkest).

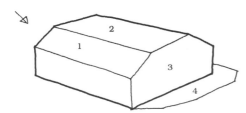

Exercise 1.40

The light source is indicated in the following drawing. Add the correct shading to the areas of the objects.

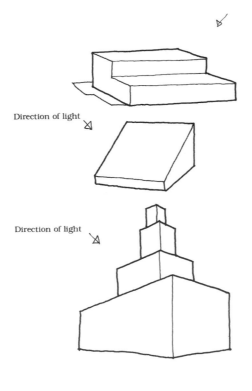

Direction of light

Direction of light

Curved Surfaces

Shading a curved surface is very much like shading a plane surface. The only difference is that the shading gradually changes from light to dark. Curved surfaces do not have a distinct edge to separate the value tones of the shading. Gradually blend the white to gray to black shading on a curved surface. This principle applies to all curved surfaces whether the object is a pipe, a cylinder, an arm, or whatever.

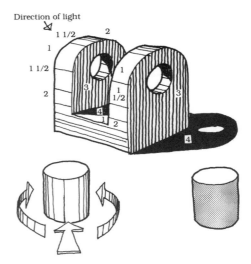

Light gradually curves around a curved surface.

Shading seems simple enough, but the concept seems to confuse many students. Look at the cylinders in the next example. The one on the left is the same as the one on the right, except that it has more lines to indicate the shading. These extra lines make the left cylinder appear to be a darker color cylinder than the one on the right.

 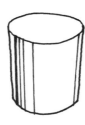

Exercise 1.41

Shade the following curved surfaces. Remember that the position of the light source (indicated in the drawings) dictates how objects should be shaded.

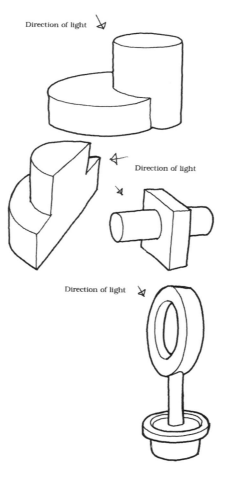

Direction of light

Direction of light

Direction of light

Reflected Light

If you look closely at objects, you will notice that reflected light is nearly always visible. The most noticeable place is on curved surfaces like a sphere or cylinder. Near the darkest part (core) of the object there is usually an area of light. Study the examples here to see how to draw this core area of reflected light.

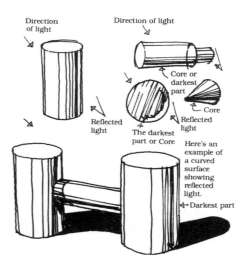

Direction of light

Direction of light

Core or darkest part

Core

Reflected light

The darkest part or Core

Reflected light

Here's an example of a curved surface showing reflected light.

Darkest part

Exercise 1.42

Shade the following objects to demonstrate reflected light.

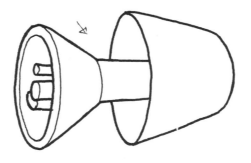

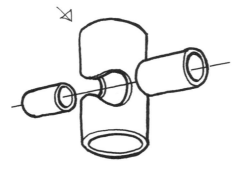

Light Against Dark

Good drawing employs the principle of continuous light against dark. The trees in the following example demonstrate this principle. The trunk of the tree goes from dark to light and back to dark again. Where the tree trunk crosses a light background, the trunk appears to be dark. Where the tree trunk crosses a dark background, the trunk appears to be light.

Make this distinction very obvious in your drawings. Begin by drawing the dark and then proceed to the lighter shades. The strongest point of emphasis is where the darkest dark or the lightest light contrasts with the surroundings. If you can lay the darkest dark against the lightest light, then you have the strongest point of contrast in the drawing. This high contrast area demands the most attention from the viewer.

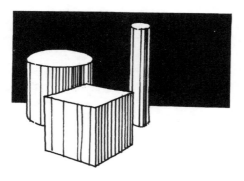

In real life, objects seldom, if ever, appear to be flat, smooth surfaces without degrees of shading. There is always a degree of variation in shading on all objects. Study smooth surfaces of things around you to see how reflections, shading, shadows, dirt, and other imperfections make those surfaces appear to have light and dark areas. You can indicate these subtle variations in your drawings by adding a few scribble lines.

Remember that in real life there is always a subtle variation in shading even on the flattest of surfaces. If you find yourself getting confused as the objects you are shading become more complex, see each object as being composed of many basic shapes. This technique will allow you to take each basic shape one at a time. Shade each shape individually, and, when finished, the whole will be shaded correctly.

Add subtle line variations to flat surfaces to make them appear more realistic.

Exercise 1.43

Without using tracing paper, copy the drawing of the trees shown on page 75 to practice the principle of continuous light against dark.

Exercise 1.44

Finish applying shading to the car in
this drawing.

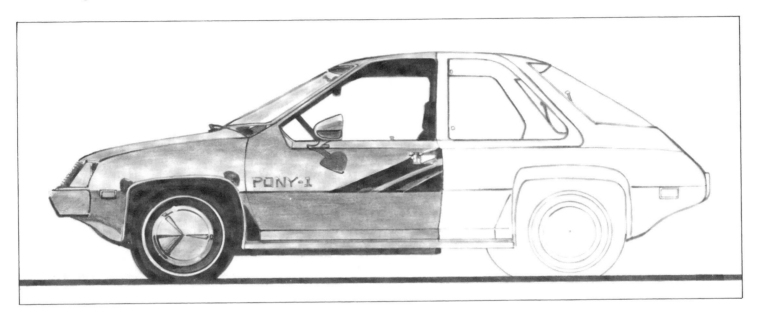

Exercise 1.45

Redraw the following objects at a larger scale than they are shown here. Apply the correct shading to each object.

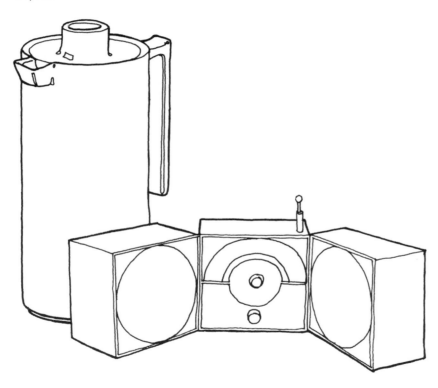

Exercise 1.46

Shade the following objects.

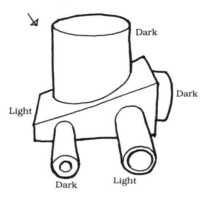

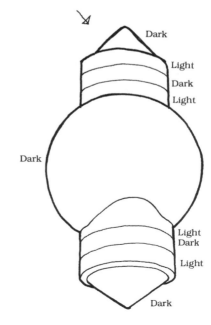

Exercise 1.47

Complete the shading on the following drawing.

Shadows

Drawing cast shadows is difficult for most people as they begin to draw. The principle of shadows is simple: A shadow is the base of a triangle formed by the direction of the light source and the object.

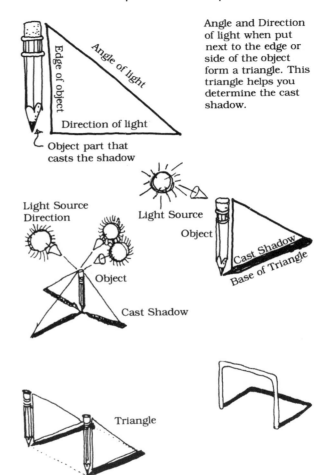

Angle and Direction of light when put next to the edge or side of the object form a triangle. This triangle helps you determine the cast shadow.

To draw a cast shadow, first determine the angle of the light source. Then draw the triangle from the edges of the object and the light source. Connect the bases of the triangles, and darken in the cast shadow area.

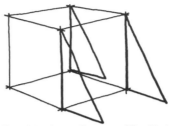

Draw triangles on all corners of the object.

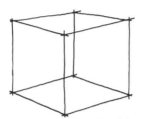

Let's take a simple cube and draw the cast shadow.

Think of the cube as being transparent so that you can see the hidden sides and edges of the cube.

Determine the angle formed by the light source and the cube side.

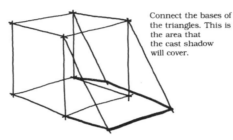

Connect the bases of the triangles. This is the area that the cast shadow will cover.

Darken in the cast shadow area.

Shadows cast from curved surfaces are created following the same process as for flat surfaces. The light source forms a triangle. You run this imaginary triangle along the curved surface to plot the area of the cast shadow.

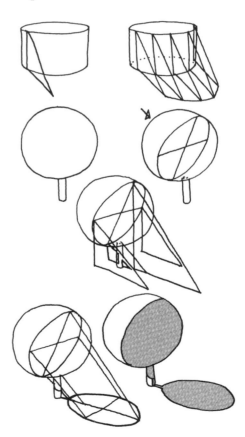

Exercise 1.48

Determine the angle of the light source, and then draw the cast shadow on the following cubes.

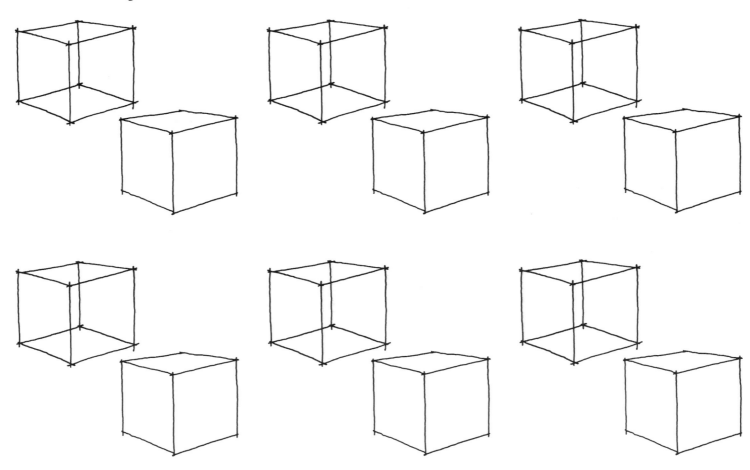

Shadows for Complicated Objects

The cast shadow of complicated objects is drawn the same way as for simple objects. You begin by determining the angle of the light source, and then draw the triangle formed by the object and the light source. The base of the triangle is the cast shadow.

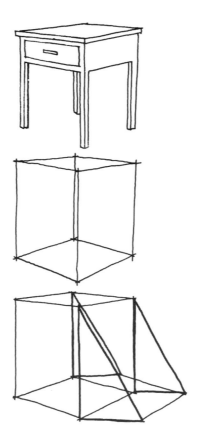

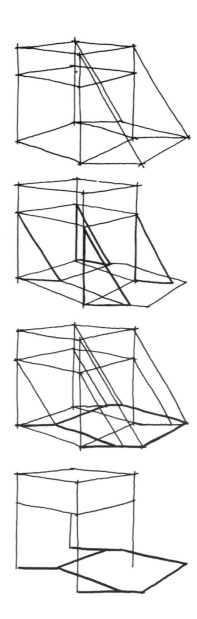

Exercise 1.49

Study the steps for drawing the cast shadow of the table used in the preceding example. Draw the shadow for the same table using a different direction of the light source.

Shadows over Objects

The shadow that falls over another object is drawn the same way as over a flat surface. Notice in the following example how the cast shadow appears to be shorter where it crosses the smaller cube. This occurs because the triangle crosses the cube higher up so that the base of the triangle is shorter.

A shadow that falls over a hole is drawn the same way, but notice in the example here that the shadow is longer due to the extra distance from the ground surface to the bottom of the hole.

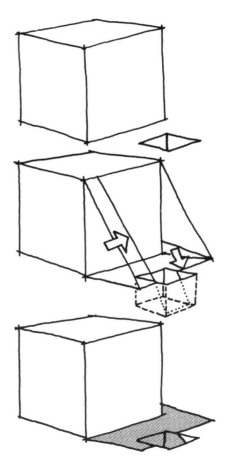

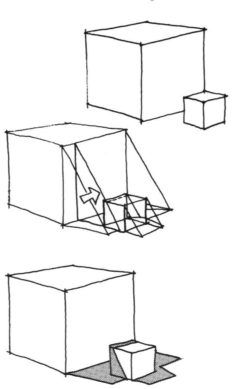

A cast shadow that falls over a curved surface is determined the same way, by finding the triangle and repeating it along the shadow casting surface.

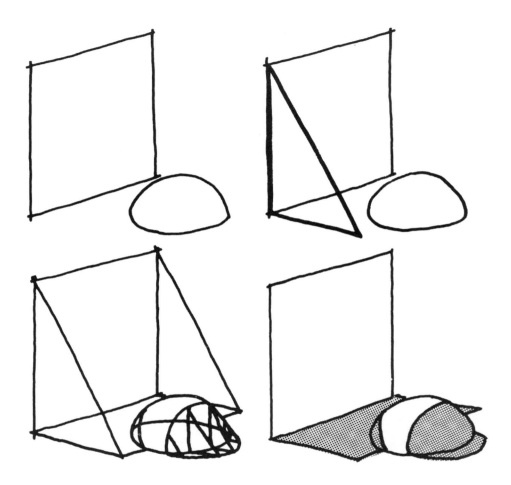

Exercise 1.50

Draw the cast shadows for these objects. They will appear quite different although they are all created using the same simple formula to create the shadows. Remember to draw the transparent edges to find the cast shadows. Also, watch the direction of the light source.

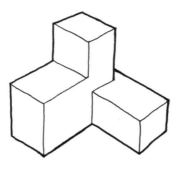

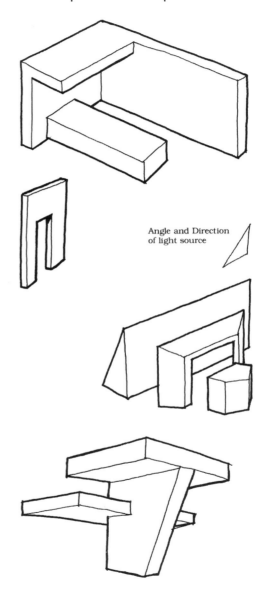

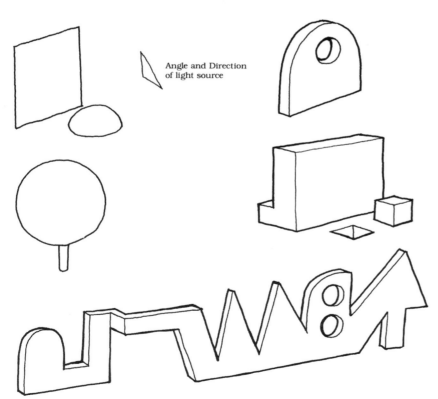

Angle and Direction of light source

Angle and Direction of light source

Exercise 1.51

In these examples, the angle and direction of the light are indicated for each object. Draw the correct cast shadow for each.

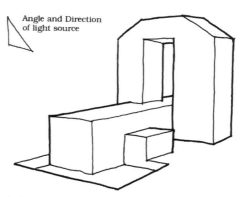

Angle and Direction of light source

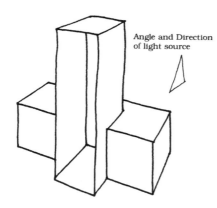

Angle and Direction of light source

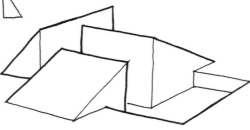

Angle and Direction of light source

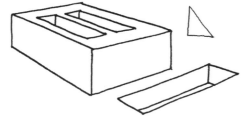

Angle and Direction of light source

Don't let this complicated shape confuse you. Refer back to the basic shading and shadow principles. Treat the object as many simple basic shapes combined to form one more complex object.

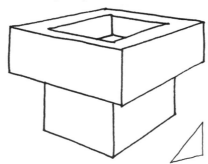

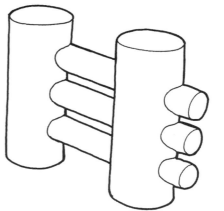

Exercise 1.52

Add shading, shadows, and other details to make this drawing more interesting.

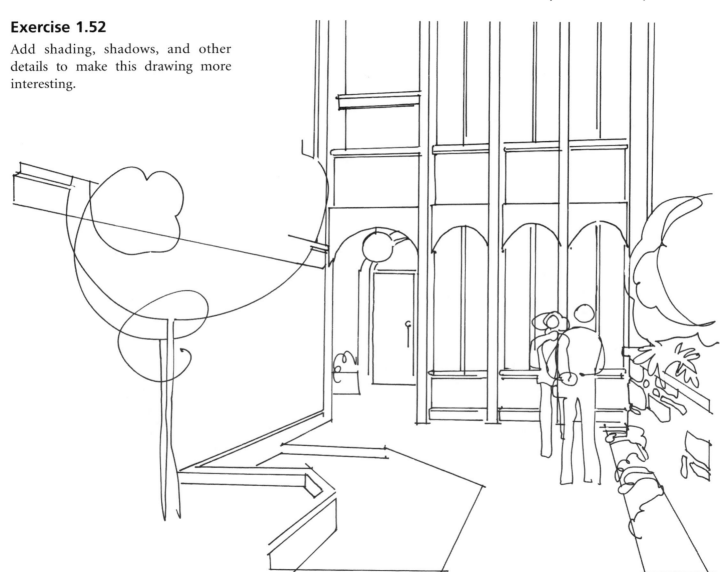

Rapid Viz Shadows and Shading

The following examples of quick sketch drawings were created by professional architects, interior designers, product designers, and landscape architects using the Rapid Viz technique. As you study the drawings, take note of the following points:

- The contrast of light against dark is used for emphasis.

- Sometimes the various tones or values are indicated by quick, loose, scribble lines to make the surfaces appear more realistic.

- Cast shadows greatly enhance the drawings.

- Sometimes drawings are created totally as degrees of shadow and shading with very little detail other than light and dark shading.

John M. Johansen

4

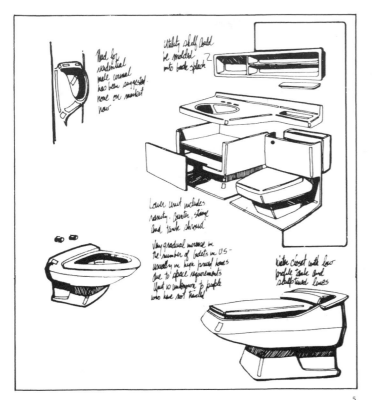

5

6

6

7   8

MODULAR

Reflections

You will find it quite helpful to learn how to draw reflections of different objects. If buildings sit near water, for example, there is a reflection of the building in the water. Many home and office products have chrome or shiny surfaces that show reflections. Glass windows and mirrors are other common reflective surfaces that will appear often in your drawings. Including accurate reflections can lend a great deal of reality to your drawings.

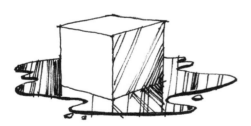

A reflection is simple to draw. It is a mirror image of the object. In the following example, notice that the house and the tree with the girl are reflected as mirror images below.

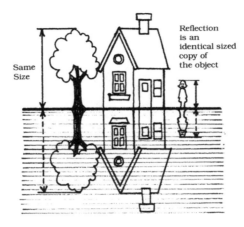

Same Size

Reflection is an identical sized copy of the object

Drawing reflections consists primarily of first drawing the object, and then plotting the reflection. Measurements of the reflection are the same as those on the object. If an object is sitting exactly on the ground or exactly on the surface of the water, the reflection begins at the baseline and is a mirror image.

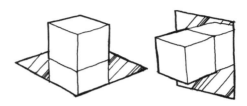

If your object sits above the reflecting surface, then you must take into account the distance from the base of the object to the reflecting surface. Measure the distance from the object to the reflecting surface, and then measure that same distance beneath the reflecting surface as in the following example.

Equal distance from object to reflective surface and reflective surface to reflected image

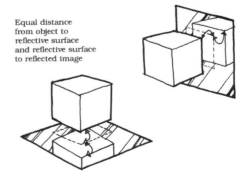

Sometimes a non-reflecting surface interferes with the reflection. In this case, draw the reflection as if it were all reflecting and then erase the part within the non-reflecting area.

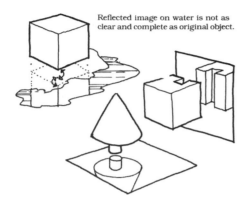

Reflected image on water is not as clear and complete as original object.

A reflection can show parts of the object that you would not see without the reflection. If you are above an object, and if that same object is above water, you will see the top of the object while the reflection will show the bottom of the object.

Exercise 1.53

These drawings are examples of partial reflections on glass, on water, and so on. Complete the reflections so you will get a feel for the process.

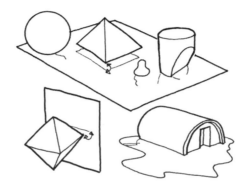

Exercise 1.54

Follow the same process to create more complicated reflections in the following drawings.

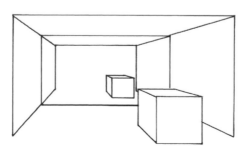

Using the first drawing as a guide, copy the image in the next drawing as a reflection in the glass surface.

Using the first drawing as a guide, copy the image in the next drawing as a reflection in the water.

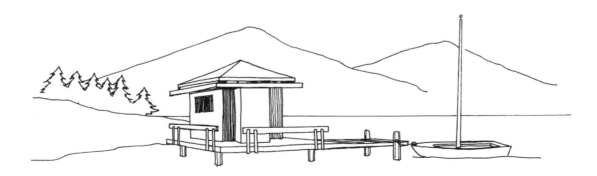

Finish drawing this partially completed waterfront scene. Be sure to include reflections and other details such as windows on buildings, surrounding buildings, people, and so on.

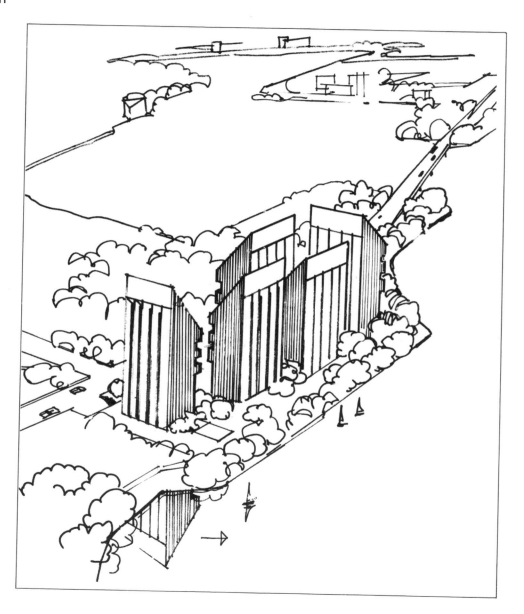

Exercise 1.55

When a shadow falls across a window, you see inside the building rather than seeing the reflection on the window. Draw the reflection in the store window shown here.

Exercise 1.56

Illustrate three bathroom fixtures. Remember that chrome on the fixtures will reflect images of other objects in the bathroom.

Exercise 1.57

Search through home decorating magazines or websites to collect at least 10 examples of photos or illustrations that show reflections. Keep these examples as the beginning of your sample file of reflected images to use as references while you practice drawing reflections.

Color

Obviously this book deals with black and white drawing. That is because color is a subject all its own. It is extremely technical and there are many factors that go into handling color well. For most architectural and product drawings, it is best to use color sparingly if at all. Use color to emphasize key points or give a little more feeling to the drawing.

Rapid Viz Principles Governing Use of Color

- In Rapid Viz drawings, add color sparingly, using no more than three levels of color. Your dominant color should be the brightest—the color that would demand the most attention. Your subordinate color should be a complementary color to the dominant one, but much less demanding. Your third color should be considerably more subdued, demanding little attention from the viewer.

- Use complementary colors. If the colors you choose contrast rather than complement each other, the viewer will be more attracted to the fight between the colors than to the colors and the overall drawing.

- Light colors advance—they punch out. Dark colors recede—they appear to be holes.

- Most shadows in objects are drawn kind of bluish in color because they often reflect the sky.

- Your paper type affects the appearance of color. Always test your drawing tool—pen, magic marker, brush, whatever—on the paper you intend to use to see what the color will be on paper.

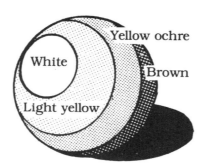

Drawing with Color

One common mistake made when drawing with color is to draw what you *think* you see rather than what you *actually* see. Colored objects usually have a variety of colors, yet people draw them as one color. Reflected color and shadows change the color of the object. Even though a wall has been painted yellow in reality, it appears to be yellow, brown, blue, black, and so on because of shadows and reflected light from surrounding objects. You must draw the wall with many colors to make it appear realistic. Draw what you actually see, not what you think you should see.

Color is like dynamite: It should be used cautiously. It should be used just in the right spot to add emphasis. Too much color can ruin your drawing.

Exercise 1.58

Draw and color the following shapes:

- A box
- A sphere
- A cone
- A cylinder

Exercise 1.59

Color the shapes made by the following combinations:

- 1 cone, 2 cylinders, and 1 cube
- 2 cubes and 1 sphere
- 1 cylinder, 1 sphere, and 1 cube

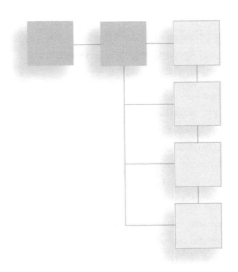

CHAPTER 2

RAPID INDICATION

Many drawings require subordinate elements that need to be there in order to set up the dominant image. These other elements are less important than the dominant image, but they plan an important role in your drawing because they set up the drawing's environment. The subordinate elements need not be complex, exact, or detailed, but they need to be there so the total drawing can be understood. These subordinate elements may be people, plants, hands, automobiles, mountains, or anything that is used to complement the key elements of the drawing.

For example, I had a student in one class who could quickly make a drawing with all elements in place. The rest of the students in the class were quite astounded that he could so quickly and easily put together total drawings. It took other students awhile to understand what was happening, but they eventually caught on. The student was quickly drawing the subordinate elements and taking additional time to make the important elements more detailed. He had visually memorized the subordinate or secondary elements that were needed for most drawings, which made it easy for him to draw their respective forms

quickly. This left him more time to concentrate on the important parts of the drawing.

This is an example of rapid indication—the process of drawing sketchy subordinate images quickly to

emphasize and complement the dominant object instead of compete with it or detract from it.

Think of this process as creating your own mental rubber stamp images. You become so familiar with drawing certain subordinate elements that the drawing process becomes automatic and consistent—as if you've used a rubber stamp to create the images.

The rapid indication process enables you to concentrate your efforts and time on the important parts of your drawing; however, the subordinate elements play an important role in the final drawing as well. They allow your main elements to be viewed in context. For example, if your drawing is of a building, it should have trees around it and people going in and out of the building. By including natural surroundings in your drawings you give the viewer a greater visual understanding of the object.

The first step of the rapid indication process is to determine the dominant object in your drawing. If it is a building, then draw it in more detail. The subordinate images—the people and foliage—can be drawn in a more sketchy and loose style to place the appropriate emphasis on the building.

The examples across the bottom of this page show an inflatable chair. The most important element in each sketch is the chair, so it is drawn with greater detail. The individuals sitting in the chairs are drawn with less detail so the viewer's focus is on the chair rather than the characters.

The last image of the woman playing guitar in the chair is an exception. This figure is overemphasized. A frequent mistake is to overemphasize figures. Be aware of this tendency so you can avoid it. The character should be indicated not emphasized in this case. Remember the object you want the viewer to focus on so you can avoid confusing the viewer.

Keys to Successful Rapid Indication

1. Keep indicated objects simple. Emphasize the critical points necessary to communicate the main element in the drawing. All other surrounding elements can be simplified even to the point of mere outline or silhouette in some drawings.

2. Subordinate all indicated objects. Put your emphasis on the major elements you are trying to communicate. Objects such as plants, people, hands, and buildings should complement the main element in the drawing.

3. Economize on indicated objects. Draw indicated objects by using the fewest lines, shapes, and parts necessary. Spend your time on the important dominant elements in the drawing. Create the indicated parts as quickly as possible.

People

People or figures are one of the most important and frequently used subordinate elements used in drawings. People add life, visual interest, and scale to your drawings. As shown in the following example, figures can be created using many different styles. There is no one set kind of figure indication that will work for all drawings. The process used to draw the figures is similar for all the drawings, but the details vary. Thus, the people appear different in each example. The purpose of your drawing, your artistic abilities, your time, and your interests will determine the appropriate kind of indicated figures for your drawings.

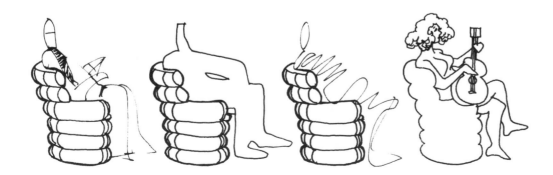

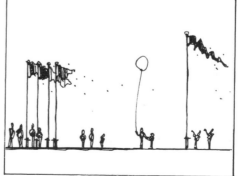

Hands

Human hands are one of the most difficult parts of the body to draw correctly. Drawing hands can be tedious, difficult, and time consuming; however, rapidly indicating hands in not difficult.

These three "tricks" will help you draw hands using rapid indication:

1. Don't draw everything. Just the outer edge and a few key lines make a hand. Details must be drawn correctly if they are included; therefore, it is best to only include essential lines and no more. You can stylize the hand to further simplify the hand.

2. What the hand does is the reason for the hand. Keep the emphasis on the actions the hand is doing rather than the hand itself.

3. Draw from life. Take photos or have someone pose in the position you want to draw. If you don't draw from life, chances are that your drawing won't look right.

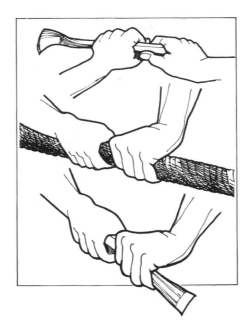

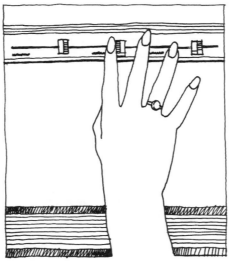

Plants and Foliage

The key to quickly drawing plants and foliage is to know the basic shape of the plant and then to use the different line techniques shown to complete the plant. The secret is to draw the "feel" of the plant and not the detail.

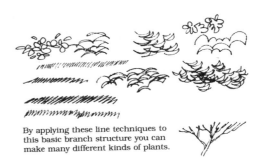

By applying these line techniques to this basic branch structure you can make many different kinds of plants.

The basic shape of the trees shown is a circle. The different kinds of trees are illustrated by the different line techniques.

Indoor plants are created the same as all other foliage. First, learn the shape of the plant, and then use various line techniques to indicate different plant varieties.

Ground cover

Ground cover is drawn by using different kinds of lines. The lines indicate varying textures, but detail is left to the viewer to imagine.

The drawings on this page evolve through different stages. The same basic kind of tree or plant is shown in varying degrees of abstraction and detail or lack of detail.

You will find that arrows can aid you in creating drawings that communicate concepts. For this reason you should become comfortable and familiar with drawing different styles of arrows. While arrows are a simple object, there are endless varieties that you can create. As you can see in these examples, there are straight arrows, curved arrows, large arrows, small arrows, fat arrows, wavy arrows, three-dimensional arrows, arrows that spin, arrows that turn, arrows that explode out of boxes, and more. Having a variety of arrow styles in your drawing repertoire will visually enhance your drawings.

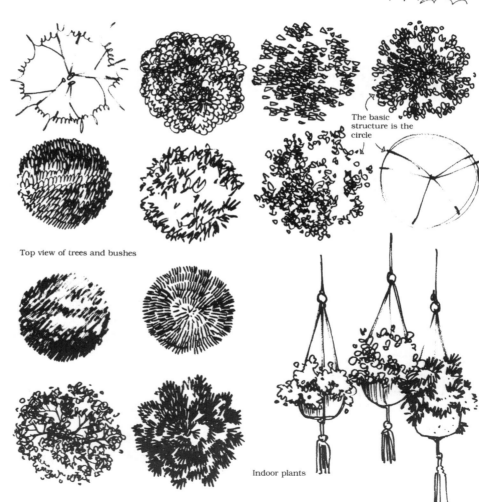

The basic structure is the circle

Top view of trees and bushes

Indoor plants

Deciduous Trees

Coniferous Trees

Plants in containers

Bushes

Lettering

Another frequently used rapid indication element is lettering. You will want to know how to indicate different styles of alphabets and letterforms. Once you learn how alphabet styles differ, you can quickly indicate a kind of lettering by imitating the basic design of that letterform.

I highly recommend that you purchase a book or two of alphabets and letterforms as a reference. A good one is *The Type Specimen Book* (Van Nostrand Reinhold Publishing). Another source is to request catalogs from lettering companies. These catalogs contain an excellent variety of different letter styles.

The next page shows examples of one person's lettering of several alphabet styles. By changing the size of the letters, the height of the lowercase letters, the line thickness, and so on, one person can create many different styles of lettering. The secret is consistency. The vertical and horizontal lines should be parallel. As you can see in the example, the first alphabet lacks quality. It is not consistent; lines are not parallel; and the slant of the letters is not uniform.

ABCDEFGHIJKLMNOPQRS
TUVWXYZ!?,
1234567890'$¢%+

By tracing alphabets from type specimen books, you can add a finished look to your drawings.

ABCDEFGHIJKLMN
OPQRSTUVWXYZ
1234567890 &

ABCDEFGHIJKLMNOPQRSTUVW /\I\\/ E
XYZ 1234567890

ABCDEFGHIJKLMNOPQRSTUVW   E=
XYZ 1234567890

ABCDEFGHIJKLMNOPQRSTUVWXYZ   E=
1234567890

ABCDEFGHIJKLMNOPQRSTUVWXYZ 1234567890 E=

ABCDEFGHIJKLMNOPQRST   E=
UVWXYZ / 2 3 4 5 6 7 8 9

ABCDEFGHIJKLMNOPQRSTUVWXYZ   E=
1234567890

ABCDEFGHIJKLMNOPQRSTU   E=
VWXYZ 1234567890

These examples demonstrate different kinds of letterforms and their relationship with the drawings. The style you choose communicates its own meaning to the viewer. Selecting the appropriate letterform for your style of drawing is essential.

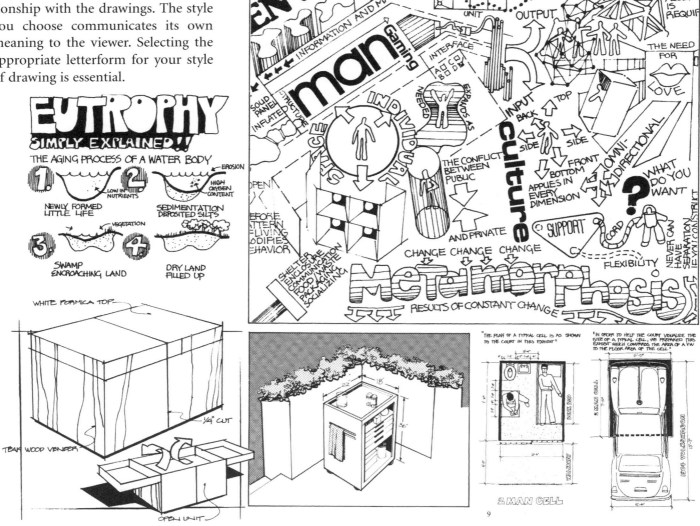

Arrows

You will find that arrows can aid you in creating drawings that communicate concepts. For this reason you should become comfortable and familiar with drawing different styles of arrows. While arrows are a simple object, there are endless varieties that you can create. As you can see in these examples, there are straight arrows, curved arrows, large arrows, small arrows, fat arrows, wavy arrows, three-dimensional arrows, arrows that spin, arrows that turn, arrows that explode out of boxes, and more. Having a variety of arrow styles in your drawing repertoire will visually enhance your drawings.

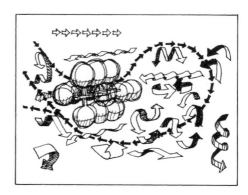

Other Indicated Elements

As you have read, there are many ways to simplify people, foliage, lettering, and the like. Other objects can be simplified in similar ways as needed for your drawings. Another frequently indicated element is the automobile. Buildings, landscapes, and mechanical parts may also be things you want or need to indicate to enhance your drawings.

In the same way that you simplified the objects in this chapter, you will develop your own style for simplifying others. Give indicated objects their essential form, but avoid including any unnecessary detail. Once these basic indications are learned they become visual clichés that you can insert into your drawings easily.

Continue to perfect ways of indication for the objects you draw often. Trying to originate new objects for each drawing is a waste of time. Develop your own mental toolbox of "rubber stamp" indicated elements. Gather your ideas from other people's work in magazines and books. Use their drawings as a springboard to help you develop your own indicated objects. Use these ideas for inspiration to improve your toolbox and your drawings.

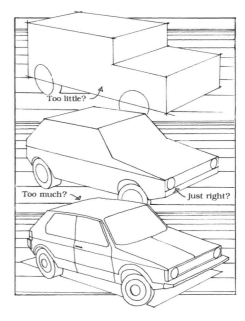

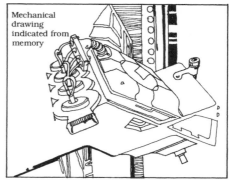

Exercises

The following exercises are designed to help you better understand and apply the principles of rapid indication in your drawings.

Exercise 2.1

Many beginners have the tendency to overdraw human figures making them appear awkward in the drawing. The following are typical examples of figure styles used by designers and architects to represent people. Draw five more figures in the style started on each line in the following example.

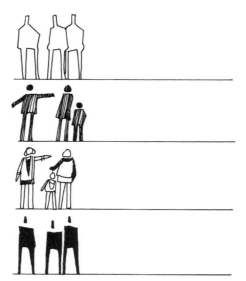

Exercise 2.2

The two environments in the following drawings look austere, lifeless, and empty because there are no people shown in them. When drawing human environments, it is critical to include people in your drawing.

Use tracing paper to redraw the two environments shown on the following page, but include figures of people. Experiment with different arrangements and figure styles until you feel that you have found a look that best complements the environment.

Exercise 2.3

Through my own experience I have developed an easy method to quickly draw a person (see page 114). I begin by drawing a square, which is the torso of the person. On top of the square draw a flattened triangle with an oval above it to create the shoulders and head. Below the square draw two more squares of equal size for hips. Add cylinders below the small squares for legs. Combine the elements and modify as appropriate for your drawing as shown in the following examples.

Many figures are started in the images shown on page 116. Place tracing paper over the images and evolve the figures into the kind of person that you want. Create any style of figure, but experiment with various styles to see which works best for you.

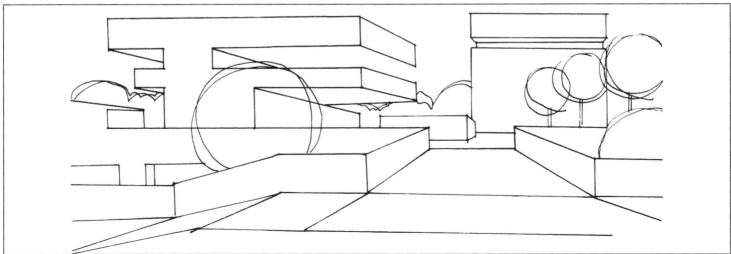

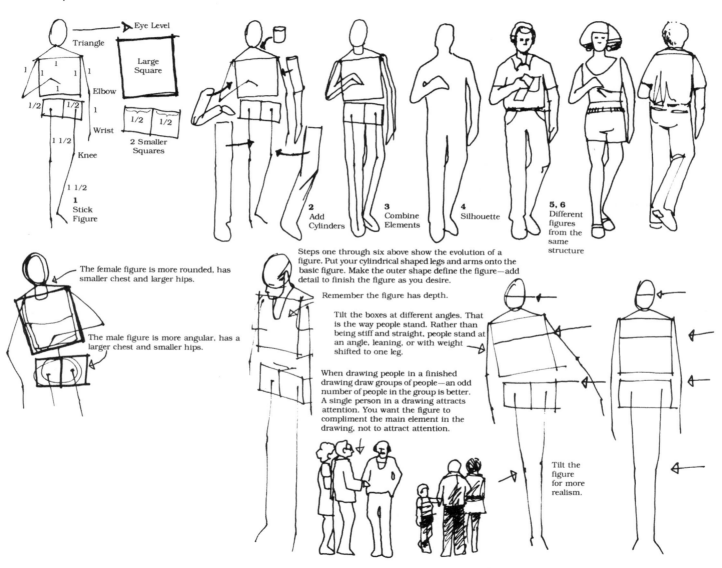

Eye Level

Triangle

Large Square

Elbow

Wrist

2 Smaller Squares

Knee

1 Stick Figure

2 Add Cylinders

3 Combine Elements

4 Silhouette

5, 6 Different figures from the same structure

The female figure is more rounded, has smaller chest and larger hips.

The male figure is more angular, has a larger chest and smaller hips.

Steps one through six above show the evolution of a figure. Put your cylindrical shaped legs and arms onto the basic figure. Make the outer shape define the figure—add detail to finish the figure as you desire.

Remember the figure has depth.

Tilt the boxes at different angles. That is the way people stand. Rather than being stiff and straight, people stand at an angle, leaning, or with weight shifted to one leg.

When drawing people in a finished drawing draw groups of people—an odd number of people in the group is better. A single person in a drawing attracts attention. You want the figure to compliment the main element in the drawing, not to attract attention.

Tilt the figure for more realism.

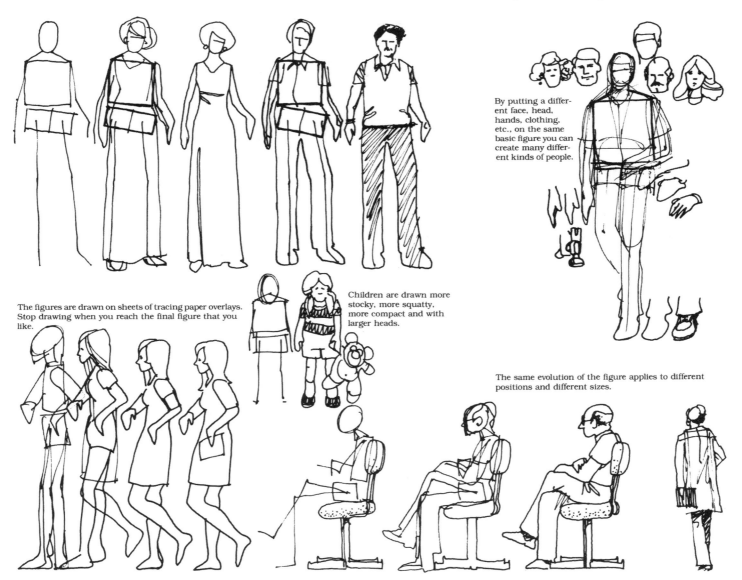

By putting a different face, head, hands, clothing, etc., on the same basic figure you can create many different kinds of people.

The figures are drawn on sheets of tracing paper overlays. Stop drawing when you reach the final figure that you like.

Children are drawn more stocky, more squatty, more compact and with larger heads.

The same evolution of the figure applies to different positions and different sizes.

Exercise 2.4

Human figures help to establish scale in drawings. By placing a person next to the object, you communicate to your viewer the size of the dominant object.

Use the following examples of scale to create your own drawings of people next to pens to indicate the scale of the pens in your drawing.

Exercise 2.5

Draw a hand using the clippers shown in the following example. Use tracing paper to draw the clippers if needed.

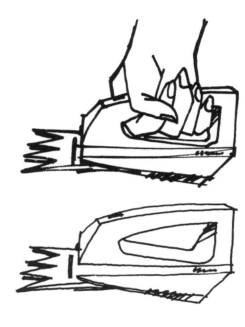

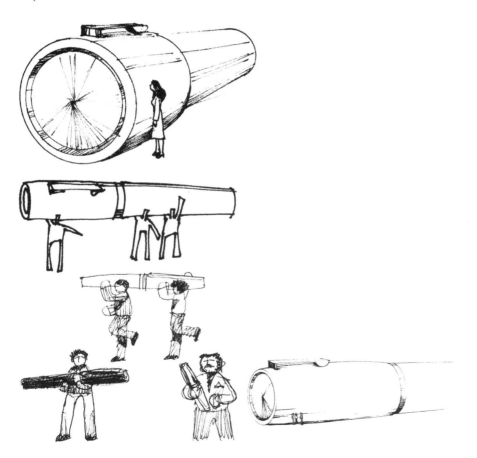

Exercise 2.6

Draw two hands holding a rod.

Exercise 2.7

Draw a hand pushing a button.

Exercise 2.8

The following building lacks pizzazz. The absence of people makes the drawing appear sterile and uninviting. Use tracing paper to redraw the building and add people to it. Be sure to stylize and simplify the figures so they do not demand too much viewer attention. Remember, the building is the dominant element in this drawing—the figures are the subordinate elements. Add other subordinate, complementary elements to the drawing such as foliage, cars, or whatever you feel works.

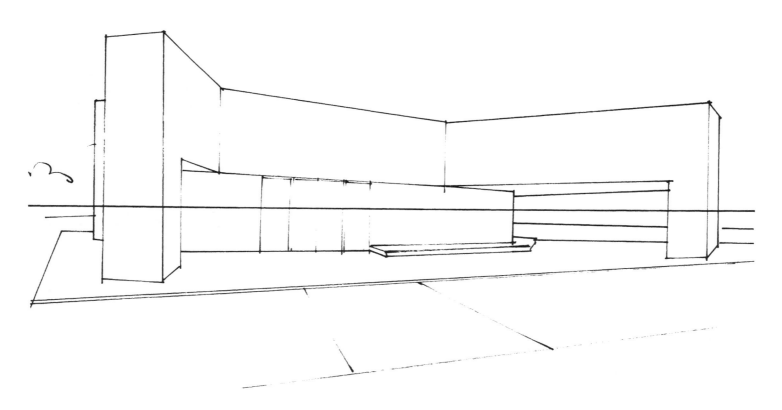

Exercise 2.9

Fill in this page with different styles of arrows, including positive arrows (black arrows against white background) and negative arrows (white arrows against dark background).

Exercise 2.10

Imagine you have just been commissioned by your city to supply the design for the soon-to-be built monument "Homage to the Cube". Make your version of the monument shown in the sketch on page 120 more appealing by adding people, plants, whatever you feel is necessary, but without changing the monument shape or design.

Exercise 2.11

The example on page 121 is a rough drawing of a clinic waiting room. Use your design talents to make the drawing look inviting. Use tracing paper overlays to finish the drawing. Add rapidly indicated elements to enhance the drawing.

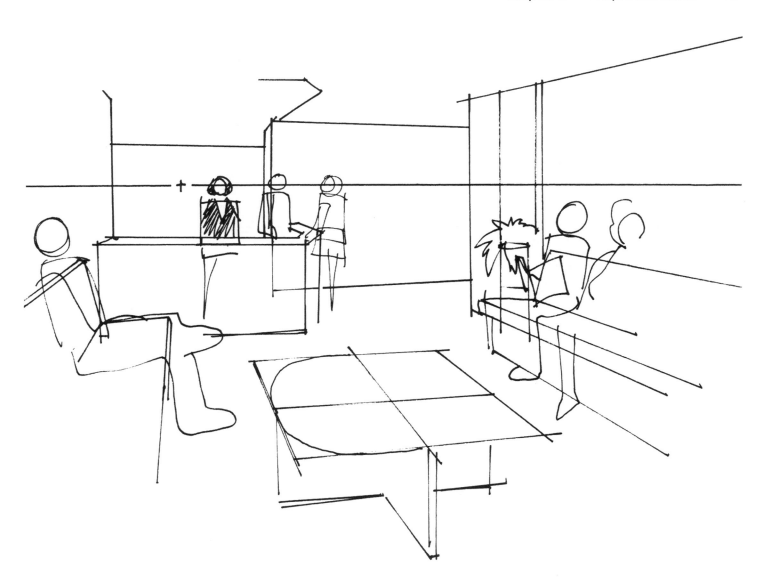

Exercise 2.12

To practice your lettering, copy the Gettysburg Address in its entirety in a style of alphabet that you like. Use tracing paper to use these lines to guide you. Your hand will ache, but your lettering will improve greatly with practice.

"Fourscore and seven years ago our fathers brought forth on this continent a new nation, conceived in liberty and dedicated to the proposition that all men are created equal. Now we are engaged in a great civil war, testing whether that nation or any nation so conceived and so dedicated can long endure. We are met on a great battlefield of that war. We have come to dedicate a portion of that field as a final resting-place for those who here gave their lives that that nation might live. It is altogether fitting and proper that we should do this. But in a larger sense, we cannot dedicate, we cannot consecrate, we cannot hallow this ground. The brave men, living and dead who struggled here have consecrated it far above our poor power to add or detract. The world will little note nor long remember what we say here, but it can never forget what they did here. It is for us the living rather to be dedicated here to the unfinished work which they who fought here have thus far so nobly advanced. It is rather for us to be here dedicated to the great task remaining before us--that from these honored dead we take increased devotion to that cause for which they gave the last full measure of devotion--that we here highly resolve that these dead shall not have died in vain, that this nation under God shall have a new birth of freedom, and that government of the people, by the people, for the people shall not perish from the earth."

CHAPTER 3

THE VISUALIZATION PROCESS

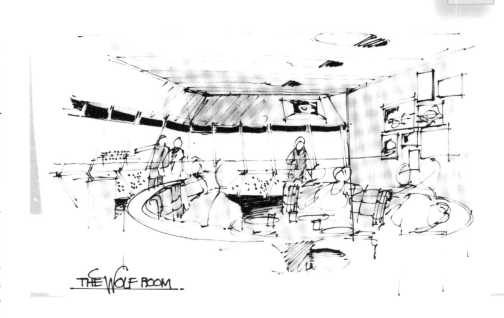

THE WOLF ROOM

The *visualization process* is the process of evolving a thought, idea, concept, or image into a finished drawing. This process is rapid development and refinement of an idea to a finished form. It involves definite steps and key concepts within each step that must be done if Rapid Viz is to be successful.

Rapid Viz is a useful sales tool in any profession. Consider as an example an architect friend of mine. He has created a large company that provides architectural renderings for various architectural firms through the nation. He attributes the growth and success of his company largely to the fact that he can go into an architect's office and convince the architect that a strong visual presentation of the proposed building will aid the architect. If that architect can show the client what the building is going to look like, there is a much better chance of getting the job and satisfying the client. My friend claims that his ability to rapidly visualize a building, in essence, to speak in visuals to the architect, aids him in landing work. As he talks to an architect about the importance of showing a client the building, my friend can draw out what he is talking about. As he draws it quickly before the architect's eyes, he gets a client and he sells a service. Using the same principle, if an architect can rapidly visualize before the client's eyes, then the architect can sell a service.

No matter what line of work you are in, if you can communicate a clear, concise message to your audience and present your concepts well, you are better off. The Rapid Viz techniques enable you to present yourself and your concepts clearly, effectively, and easily.

Key Steps in the Rapid Viz Process

The common error made by many people is to think that they can go to the finished drawing without any intermediary steps. It is impossible to arrive at a finished drawing without going through each step of the process. It may seem slow or strange, but step-by-step is the most efficient way to reach the finished product.

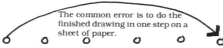

The common error is to do the finished drawing in one step on a sheet of paper.

The rapid viz process is key steps done rapidly on overlayed sheets of tracing paper.

An attempt to skip to the end of a finished drawing without progressively solving the problems along the way only creates more problems in the end. I've watched as students spend as many as 30 hours perfecting a single drawing. They would erase and rework the drawing trying to make it just right. They tried to make the leap from a half-formed idea to a finished form drawing, which just doesn't work.

By rapidly performing each step and considering all the important points in each step, it is possible, with practice, to achieve a finished drawing faster and with greater accuracy.

Develop Your Speed

Speed is important when refining the drawing. You should push yourself to draw as rapidly as possible. People learn to read faster by pushing themselves beyond their limits. In the process, they read very fast, often so fast that they do not comprehend or remember what they are reading. But when they slow down again, they usually slow down to a reading speed that is faster than where they originally started. The same principle works with drawing. You need to push yourself to draw faster than you normally do. When you slow down again you will find that your new *normal* speed has actually increased. As you push yourself faster and faster your speed gradually improves to the point where you can draw quickly while maintaining your accuracy.

You actually may be surprised to find that speed improves the visual appearance of your drawings. They will look fresher as you learn to drawn them more rapidly.

In the cold hard world of business, time is money. If you are an architect, engineer, designer, or whatever, the firm you work for will not keep you if you can't produce a good product quickly.

The following graph shows a time efficiency curve. The message conveyed by the curve is that you get to a point in your drawings where it takes considerable time to gain any improvement. When you first start a drawing every bit of time makes a great deal of improvement in the drawing, but as the drawing progresses to a more finished stage, it takes more and more time to make any visible improvement in the drawing. You

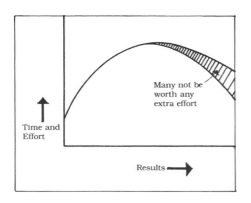

Many not be worth any extra effort

Time and Effort

Results ➡

need to learn when you have passed the point of efficiency—the point of diminishing returns. Stop when you are spending too much time for the good derived.

One way to guard against inefficient use of time is to determine in the beginning what is needed for your drawing. If you can accomplish your goal by drawing quickly on a scrap of paper, why do more? If detail is important to convey the idea, use detail. If detail is not necessary, then don't go to the bother of including unnecessary detail. You can become more efficient by deciding what is needed, drawing to that point, and not doing more.

Know Your Audience

When creating visuals for communicating or presenting an idea, consider your audience carefully. Who is the audience? Why are they there? What do you want them to know? What do they need to know? How are you going to tell them? Why should they know it?

Don't draw what you want to see. Draw what your audience wants to see. If you don't consider your audience, your visual presentation won't work.

For example, the following series of drawings depicts a man putting rocks into a mining cart. This visual was used in Africa. It didn't work. The visual was supposed to tell workers in a mine that they were to pick up debris on the track and put it in a cart to haul it away. However, the African mineworkers were used to reading things in the opposite direction (from right to left) as was their native custom. The result was that the tracks became cluttered with debris because the workers thought that what was meant by the visual was to gather up the rocks, take the rocks to the track, put the rocks on the track, and leave them there. The miscommunication was caused because the visuals were drawn from the communicator's point of view, not from the audience's point of view or reference.

10

When using visuals in a presentation, always consider the point of view of the audience. That is the most important factor in the success of a presentation.

Follow the Process

Keep in control by following the Rapid Viz process step by step. Do not try to skip ahead or overcorrect.

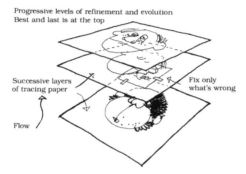

Progressive levels of refinement and evolution
Best and last is at the top

Successive layers of tracing paper

Fix only what's wrong

Flow

By following the process outlined throughout this chapter your drawing will evolve through successive layers of tracing paper. Each successive drawing is done quickly using transparent sheets of tracing paper. Fix only what is wrong with the previous drawing. Let the best of the drawing rise to the top and the worst parts fall away with each new drawing.

As you progress from layer to layer, focus on improving the following elements of your drawing:

- whole to parts
- known to unknown
- simple to complex
- coarse to refined
- rough to finished
- vague to clear
- small to large

The Rapid Viz Process

The Rapid Viz process can be divided into the following three stages:

> Stage 1: Thumbnails
>
> Stage 2: Transparencies
>
> Stage 3: Final Drawing

A series of goals or key concepts applies to each stage.

Stage 1: Thumbnails

During the thumbnail stage, you make quick, small idea sketches to visualize the central concepts—the basic idea of how you're going to put the drawing together. Thumbnails show very little detail. Their primary purpose is to set the stage for the final drawing by solving conceptual problems—basic ideas, feelings, and relationships between elements. The thumbnail stage is a quick, rough sketch done to scale but small—about the size of your thumb, hence the name.

You can solve many of the problems at thumbnail scale before moving to the next step. It is much easier to work at this small size to solve the problems rather than full scale. You should learn to play with things, to defer judgment, and to conceive many different thumbnail drawings, each one a further clarification of the previous one.

Many critical decisions are made during this stage. The following images are several examples in which thumbnails have played an important part in the development process. These examples demonstrate the wide range of styles that thumbnails can take.

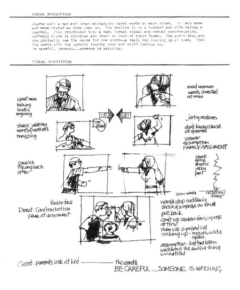

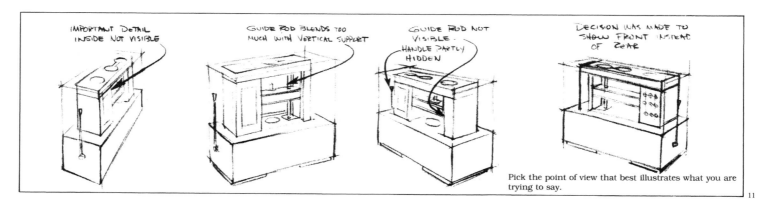

IMPORTANT DETAIL INSIDE NOT VISIBLE

GUIDE ROD BLENDS TOO MUCH WITH VERTICAL SUPPORT

GUIDE ROD NOT VISIBLE. HANDLE PARTLY HIDDEN

DECISION WAS MADE TO SHOW FRONT INSTEAD OF REAR

Pick the point of view that best illustrates what you are trying to say.

The goals of the thumbnail stage are:

- To create small drawings that enable you to create multiple versions of the object to find the best solution.

- To determine the point of view of the drawing.

- To find the best outer proportion for the drawing.

- To solve negative/positive shape relationships.

- To become aware of the perceptual tendencies of the viewer toward your drawing.

- To solve value relationships by working from dark to light values.

Quantity

Because thumbnails are small, quickly drawn, conceptual drawings, you can draw many until you find a solution to your problem. The more ideas you can put on paper, the better your chance to find an appropriate solution.

The natural tendency is to start with typical solutions that should work and then proceed to more unique and outlandish solutions as you create more thumbnails. The best solutions often come in the later thumbnails—not the early ones. Defer judgment to allow yourself to have a mind free of prejudices as you work. The more possibilities you can come up with, the greater your chance to find a workable solution. Don't be afraid to

combine ideas from many thumbnails into one good solution.

Outer Proportion

To understand outer proportion, first consider the *picture plane*. The picture plane is the shape of the paper, the final overall proportion that you have to work with. It's a flat surface through which the picture is seen. This plane establishes the comparative relationships with all other lines, planes, directions, and movements within its borders. The picture plane is the basis for judging how the elements will work.

The picture is limited entirely by this surface. It is a restriction that you have to live with—a basic shape that dictates and sets the bounds for your drawing. This picture frame is the artificially frozen image you have to deal with, and the shape of it affects what's in it. Your drawing will only look good if it is positioned correctly within the drawing area.

Order of Importance

You cannot emphasize all parts of the drawing. Some things are subordinate to other things. You must decide which things are most important in the drawing and which things are less important. This order of importance determines how you will draw certain elements and where you will position things.

I find that if I assign three levels of dominance in the drawing that I get the best results. One or two main points in the drawing are dominant. Other things are subordinate to the dominant elements. Still other elements are subordinate to everything else.

Point of View

Point of view is the position in space from where you view the image you plan to draw. You must decide the point of view—at, above, or below eye level—before you begin to draw.

Once you have determined the appropriate eye level, you must decide where to place elements within the drawing. As a general rule, we all have a natural visual preference for odd divisions over even divisions. One third is generally more visually pleasing than one half. This can be deliberately imposed on your drawing by dividing it into thirds and putting the dominant elements, or points of emphasis, within those thirds.

Use a grid matrix to aid in correct placement of elements in a drawing. This matrix should consist of hidden lines that are unseen but are always there. The matrix helps organize the elements in the drawing to give cohesiveness to the image.

Because the purpose of the matrix is to give order to the drawing, be careful not to violate the matrix. If you absolutely must break the matrix, do

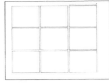

This is a sample of the grid matrix used for the layout of this book.

so only for a good reason. The grid matrix creates an organized linear quality that is felt in all well designed graphic presentations. Use the grid to control the drawing so that you can accomplish a particular goal that you are trying to reach in the drawing.

Negative/Positive Shape Relationships

Shapes are either negative (light) or positive (dark). The following example demonstrates the relationship of negative and positive shapes. In this example, the positive image of two face profiles is instantly obvious to most people. However, many people have difficulty seeing the negative image of a vase.

What do you see below?
Two heads or a vase?
One is a negative shape, the other is a positive shape.

In order for a drawing to succeed, both negative and positive shapes must be interesting. The negative shape is probably the most critical yet most often neglected as you draw. Make an effort to make the negative shape interesting. Indeed, make both the negative and the positive shapes interesting.

Value Relationships

I try to use four values in my drawings—dark, dark grey, light grey, and light. The best way to decide placement of the values is to begin with the darkest colors first and proceed to the light colors. Give the drawing punch by placing the darkest values next to the lightest values. It is important that you draw correct shading and shadows, but you can alter reality in order to achieve a desired result. The placement of different values in the drawing determines the overall design of the drawing.

Be careful to position values in the most interesting place. This will come

with practice, but as you learn to place values remember to divide space in interesting patterns and to use values to emphasize things.

Perceptual Tendencies

People have natural *perceptual tendencies*, or preferences for viewing things. People naturally tend to see visual things in common patterns. They have a tendency to look at things from left to right, the same way they are taught to read, and from top to bottom. If a circular pattern is used, people feel more comfortable seeing it in a clockwise direction.

Lines suggest various movements. Horizontal lines suggest a quiet, stable movement from left to right. The vertical line becomes very active, suggesting movement from top to bottom. A diagonal line is dynamic. It feels like it is falling down and suggests danger.

Be conscious of these natural perceptual tendencies of people, so you can employ them in your drawing.

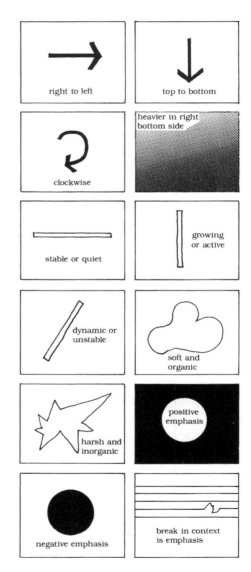

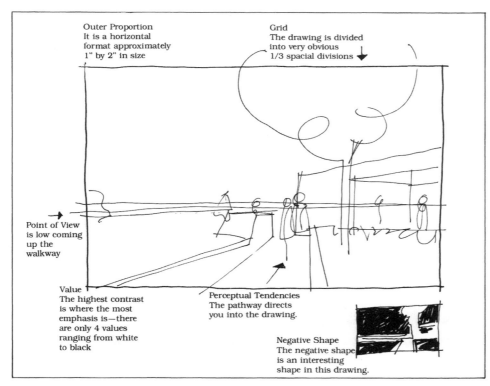

Outer Proportion
It is a horizontal
format approximately
1" by 2" in size

Grid
The drawing is divided
into very obvious
1/3 spacial divisions

Point of View
is low coming
up the
walkway

Value
The highest contrast
is where the most
emphasis is—there
are only 4 values
ranging from white
to black

Perceptual Tendencies
The pathway directs
you into the drawing.

Negative Shape
The negative shape
is an interesting
shape in this drawing.

Stage 2: Transparencies

The second stage of the drawing process is the transparency stage. In this stage you create the first full-size sketch. The problems of design, division of space, negative and positive shapes, and the like have been resolved during the thumbnail allowing you to focus on converting the thumbnail to the full scale size and refining the drawing into a finished form. This transparent stage is where you work out the basic relationship between the parts.

The goals of the transparency stage are:

- To transfer the drawing from the small thumbnail to the larger finished size.

- To begin with transparent shapes and evolve to actual drawing by tracing the drawing again and again.

- To determine emphasis and use detail, contrast, and the like to emphasize those things you want emphasized in the drawing.

- To add the necessary detail to the elements in the drawing to make a finished drawing.

- To correct errors as you proceed from transparency to transparency.

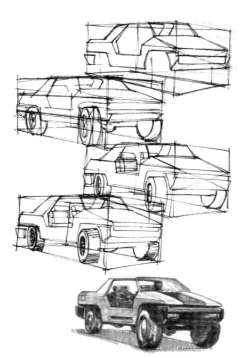

Redraw at Full Scale

The first step is to transfer your drawing from thumbnail to full scale. Once you know that the thumbnail is designed correctly, then duplicate the rough form full scale. There are many ways to enlarge your thumbnail to full scale. (Refer to Chapter 1 for more on the grid method.)

One thing to remember is that you cannot draw something if you do not know what it looks like. You can't drink from an empty cup; you can't draw from an empty head. If you don't have the image of what you are drawing firmly planted in your mind, then you must have an object or image to look at to aid you in drawing the object correctly.

Refine the Drawing

To this point you have transferred the thumbnail sketch to a full-size drawing. What you need to do now is refine the drawing. Lay a transparent sheet on top of the drawing. Redraw the same image again. It is much easier to refine by a transparent process than it is to erase and work over the original. With this method you can drop out the things that you don't want or retain and improve the things that you do want.

It could take only one transparent tracing after the full-scale blowup or it might take 10 or 20 tries to get the drawing just right. It is easier and faster to redraw using transparent tracing than it is to rework the original.

Transparent Shapes

Once you have a full-scale drawing, the next step is to correct the drawing. Define the basic shapes. You will have spheres, cubes, and cylinders that are the beginnings of what they will eventually become—buildings, people, and so forth. Correct the perspective so that the appropriate lines converge at vanishing points, the lines that should be parallel are parallel, and so forth. One way to make this drawing correct is to include the hidden lines that will not show in the final drawing. What I mean by hidden lines are the edges, the corners, and the sides of the building that will not be seen in the finished drawing. Drawing the hidden lines as though the building or object appears to be transparent allows you to be sure the elements are drawn correctly.

There are certain essential points in any drawing. The corner of a building, the point of a gable of a building, or the base of an electronic receiver are examples of these critical points in a drawing. They define the limits of what you are drawing. If you put an obstruction in front of one of these important points, it is difficult for the viewer to imagine how the object goes. It is important to have certain key points in the drawing exposed to help the viewer understand what is happening in the drawing.

Emphasis

The basic principle of emphasis is to have something out of context. That is, you emphasize the dominant elements by making them different from the surroundings. For example, a circle among squares, a bump in a long straight line, a light speck against a dark surface, or detailed shapes against plain surfaces are all examples of something being emphasized.

Change tends to attract our attention. These changes create emphasis.

For example, if the emphasis in a drawing is a certain building, put your dark against lights and your details there. The points of change will draw attention and contribute to the viewer seeing that building.

Be sure to emphasize the dominant elements and de-emphasize the subordinate elements. If, as in the previous example, a building is the dominant element in your drawing, give the building the most details, the brightest colors, the most contrast, and so forth so the viewer's attention is drawn to the building. The subordinate elements—the trees, the people, the surroundings of the building—should be less detailed, show less contrast, feature less interesting colors, and so on.

Errors

As you work with a drawing it will probably become close to your heart. You will begin to overlook glaring and obvious mistakes because you are working so closely with it. I have drawn buildings before that looked just fine to me after working on them

for two or three hours, only to have other people ask me why I had made such obvious mistakes. For example, the building had walls that slanted or other obvious mistakes. I had become so attached to the drawing that I had overlooked these mistakes. This is why it is essential that you have a way to check your drawing to make sure you have not made some glaring errors.

One of the most effective ways to check for errors is to get another point of view from which to see your drawing. Some ways you can do that are:

- Turn your drawing upside-down.
- Hold your drawing in front of a mirror.
- Ask a friend to look at it.
- Put your drawing across the room at a distance from you and look at the drawing.
- Leave your drawing and then return to it a day or a week later. The time lapse will enable you to look at the drawing with "new eyes".

Upon discovering mistakes in your drawing you will need to decide what warrants correcting and what is just overkill. If the mistake isn't important to the purpose of the drawing, you may not need to spend the time correcting it. If the mistake detracts from the drawing, it is worth the effort to correct it.

When drawing in three dimensions keep in mind the following points:

- Bigger things appear closer and smaller things appear farther away.
- Place objects in front of or behind other objects so that overlapping occurs to give a more realistic feeling of depth.

- Lines converge in the distance as the objects move away from you.
- Place a cutting edge around the outside edge of objects.

Stage 3: The Final Drawing

In this stage you evolve the drawing into the final form that the viewer will see. This time your emphasis is to give the drawing a freshness and strive for viewer involvement. Some drawings will go through many transparencies and be quite elaborate before getting to this stage, and others will get there relatively quickly.

The goals of the final drawing stage are:

- To begin with transparent shapes and evolve to the actual final drawing.
- To determine appropriate use of color in your drawing.
- To deliberately backtrack your drawing to involve the viewer.
- To use line weight to make your drawing more visually appealing.
- To mount your drawing for presentation to your audience.

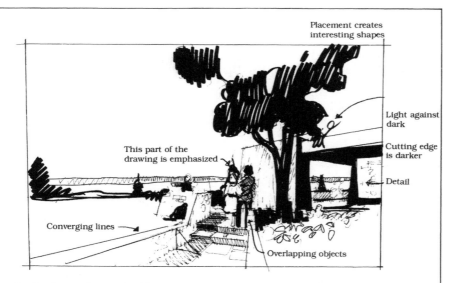

As you evolve this drawing through the different stages, you have worked it to make it more correct, but you may find that your drawing has that look of being overdone. This is one of the most common mistakes that people make as they begin to draw. They fiddle to the point that the drawing is overdone. I expect that, in the beginning, this will happen to you. That's all right, because in the next stage I will show you how to loosen up the drawing. I will show you how to get some viewer involvement with your drawing—how to give it more appeal. So don't worry about making it overdone at this stage. Worry about making it *correct*.

Context

The value of the final drawing is its ability to communicate the message that you want your drawing to convey to the viewer. The final touches you make to the drawing should be refined in accordance with the message you want to convey. You should strive for the image to communicate its message to the viewer in a loose, free, and spontaneous manner.

Color

You may determine that some color will help your drawing. Remember to be selective and use color sparingly. A little color at strategic points should be sufficient. Rapid Viz line drawings do not need more than three colors—a bright color for the most important part of the drawing, a more subdued secondary color that complements the main color, and a very subdued third color. Don't be so splashy with color that your drawing looks like a circus—unless you are drawing a circus, of course.

Backtrack—Developing Viewer Involvement

You have evolved your drawing and corrected your drawing so that it is complete and correct. You may want, however, to undo some of the drawing so that the viewer can become involved. You want the viewer to get the feeling that you did it rapidly—in just a few minutes—but very skillfully. You want your drawing to communicate rather than be "just another drawing."

You want your drawing to interact with the viewer so he becomes intensely involved with the drawing. One way to cause this to happen is to leave out details that the viewer must fill in from his own mind. Most people don't realize that they have a tendency to fill in things, but they do. You have heard the saying, "Roses are red, violets are…." You completed the phrase in your mind, didn't you? That's how it works with images too. The way you achieve viewer involvement in your drawing is to leave out little things here and there.

Go back to your final drawing and make a few last changes. Leave out lines, details, and other little things here and there. This will cause the viewer to become more involved with your drawing because the viewer must now fill in the details in his or her mind.

Line Quality

Another element that helps finish your final drawing is to use different densities of lines. You should use at least three kinds of lines within your drawing. You should have some hard, thick, dark lines; some medium thickness lines; and some very light, faint lines. Three different line thicknesses make your drawing livelier and more visually interesting to the viewer.

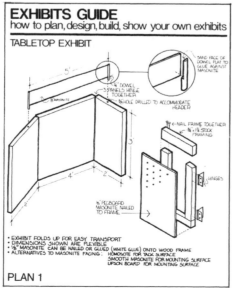

EXHIBITS GUIDE
how to plan, design, build, show your own exhibits

TABLETOP EXHIBIT

SAND FACE OF DOWEL FLAT TO GLUE AGAINST MASONITE

¼" DOWEL
3 PANELS HINGE TOGETHER
¾ HOLE DRILLED TO ACCOMMODATE HEADER

NAIL FRAME TOGETHER
¾" x 1¼ STOCK FRAMING

HINGES

⅛ PEGBOARD MASONITE NAILED TO FRAME

• EXHIBIT FOLDS UP FOR EASY TRANSPORT
• DIMENSIONS SHOWN ARE FLEXIBLE
• ⅛" MASONITE CAN BE NAILED OR GLUED (WHITE GLUE) ONTO WOOD FRAME
• ALTERNATIVES TO MASONITE FACING: HOMOSOTE FOR TACK SURFACE
                                     SMOOTH MASONITE FOR MOUNTING SURFACE
                                     UPSON BOARD FOR MOUNTING SURFACE

PLAN 1

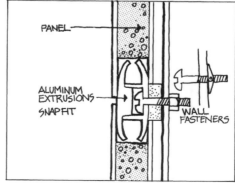

PANEL

ALUMINUM
EXTRUSIONS
SNAP FIT

WALL
FASTENERS

Mounting

When the drawing is completely finished you will need to mount it for your audience to view. This is because your drawing was completed on transparent tracing paper, which needs a backup sheet for proper viewing. The most common way to mount drawings is to cut a window out of matte board and affix the drawing behind the window; however, I do not recommend this method unless you intend to show the drawing over and over again. I prefer to use other methods that are faster and less expensive, but look just as nice for most viewing situations.

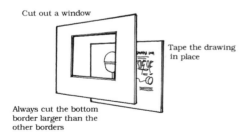

Cut out a window

Tape the drawing in place

Always cut the bottom border larger than the other borders

One easy, inexpensive method is to draw a very bold line around the outer edge of the drawing, and then simply adhere the drawing to an opaque piece of paper using staples, tape, or the like.

Another method is to use spray adhesive to adhere the drawing to a piece of matte board. Affix black photo tape, which can be purchased from a photography store, around the edge of the drawing to form a border, and cut the matte board to size.

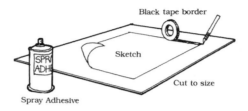

Black tape border

Sketch

Cut to size

Spray Adhesive

Presenting the Finished Drawing

The very last thing for a final drawing is to make sure that the drawing is presented under the right conditions. Make sure the style of the drawing fits the situation in which you present it. If the drawing needs to be finished, make sure you present a finished drawing. If it needs to be rough and spontaneous, then make your drawing sketchy and rough.

Try to foresee the circumstance under which the drawing will be viewed. If it is a planning meeting for a building committee, for example, you may want to keep the drawing sketchy and loose so that the people don't incorrectly assume that you have made final design decisions when you don't have the authority to do so.

When presenting your finished drawing, make sure it is of adequate size and placed in the right position. If your audience is viewing it from 50 feet away, you cannot use an 8 1/2 × 11 sheet of paper. Similarly, if you are presenting it to kindergarten students, you would not hang it 7 feet high on the wall.

I have seldom, if ever, completed a drawing that I thought was good enough. The feeling is always that something could have been done better. But there comes a point where there is no time or desire to do more. I have to quit a particular drawing and move on to other things. You probably will experience similar feelings. Don't worry—it's normal to feel that way. Keep trying because this feeling motivates you to continuously improve your abilities.

The Finished Drawing

Remember one important rule when presenting your finished drawing: the visuals used in presentation are a means to an end. We use those visuals to communicate a message or concept. They are not an end in themselves. Visuals are not meant to be hung on a wall or in a gallery for other people to see or to last forever. They are meant as a means of communication. The following final drawings demonstrate the successful application of the Rapid Viz process.

Notice areas where lines are left out—this will loosen a tight drawing.

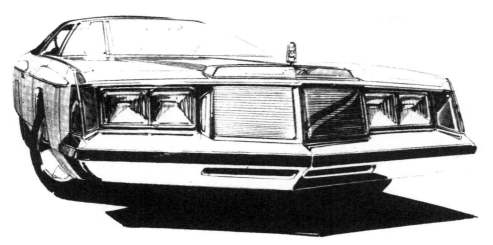

12

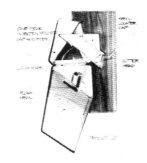

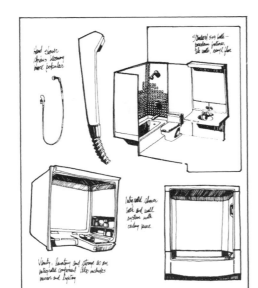

13

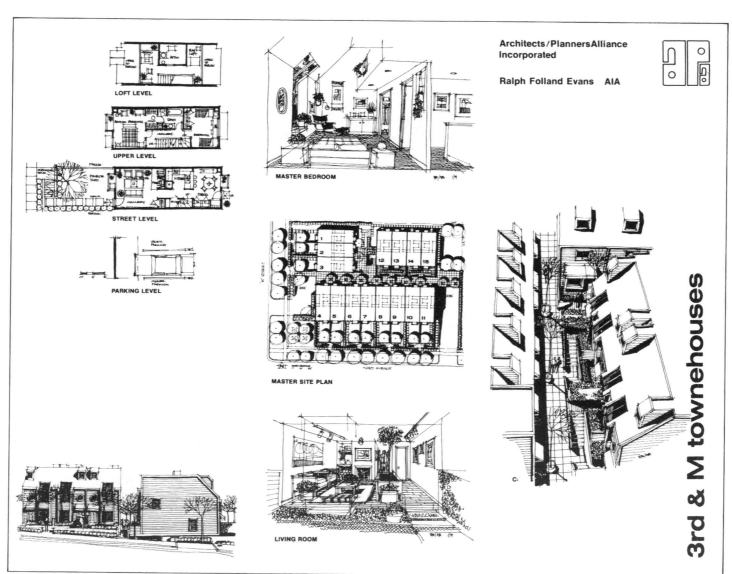

LOFT LEVEL

UPPER LEVEL

STREET LEVEL

PARKING LEVEL

MASTER BEDROOM

MASTER SITE PLAN

LIVING ROOM

Architects/Planners Alliance
Incorporated

Ralph Folland Evans   AIA

3rd & M townehouses

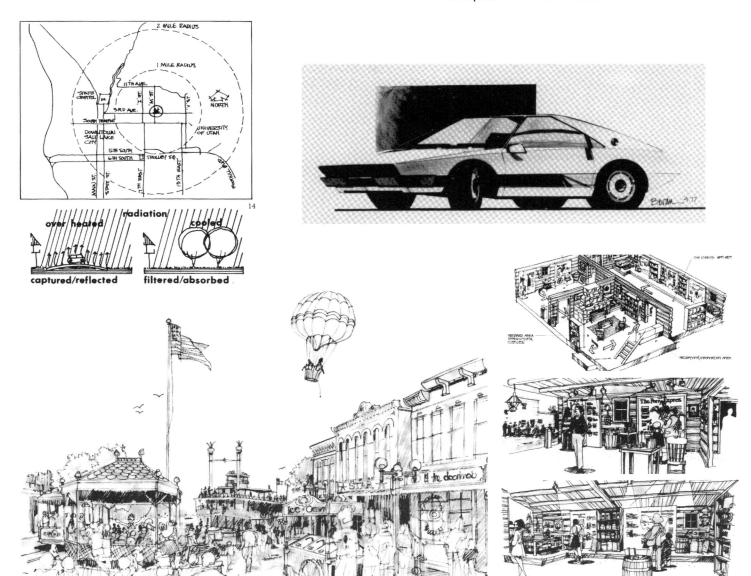

Exercises

The following exercises are designed to help you better understand and apply the skill of drawing thumbnails.

Exercise 3.1

Draw a thumbnail (no larger than 2" × 3") of any three of the following items:

- A new idea for city-wide bus stops complete with appealing landscaping.
- A modular mobile home exterior design.
- An interior for the new "Burgereater" fast food restaurant near the University campus.
- A monument to be erected at a local aquarium.
- A layout of your new business stationery.

Exercise 3.2

Draw your recommendation for improving what you consider to be the worst commercial on TV. Include at least seven segments.

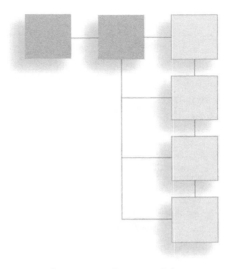

CHAPTER 4

GRAPHIC EXPRESSION

How important is it to learn to refine and expand visual potential? It's vital.

The mind thinks in pictures. It "sees" things. Where most of us fall short is in our ability to express these visual images. We benefit greatly when we learn to refine and express our visual abilities.

In this section, I hope to show you how visual abilities can be refined through *graphic expression*. Graphic expression is the conversion of thoughts, ideas, or concepts into symbols that have meaning.

In this chapter, you will learn:

- How to get more out of your symbols through the process of graphic expression of your thoughts.

- How to create your own original graphic symbols that express the message you want to communicate to your audience.

It is unfortunate that graphic expression is not taught in most schools along with writing, because graphic expression has the same widespread and valuable potential as a method of communication. For example, it is easier to draw a map than it is to write out in words all that a map can show graphically. The more effectively you use graphic expression, the more freedom and ease you will have expressing yourself.

We all use graphic expression throughout life. We use symbols to express thoughts and concepts. For example, each of the four symbols shown in the following drawing represents the concept of water.

Another example is the use of the following common symbols to express ideas or concepts.

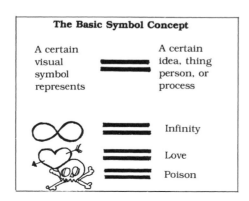

As you can see the use of symbols isn't anything new. We use symbols to convey information all the time. However, what you probably don't do is get the most of out of the symbols you use.

New Symbols

When you express yourself graphically, each thought, each concept, each message has its own set of symbols. Since most people don't learn how to make symbols, they have difficulty expressing themselves graphically. So one of the first things that you need to learn is how to make symbols. You must learn how to give meaning to symbols so that when other people see your symbols, they understand what's happening.

Applying Graphic Expression

Once you have mastered how to create graphic symbols, the use of graphic expression begins to be helpful in three basic ways.

Graphic expression is:

- A great way to communicate clear, concise messages.
- A tool to aid in learning and remembering.
- A method of expanding the mind to inspire creative thinking and realize creative potentials.

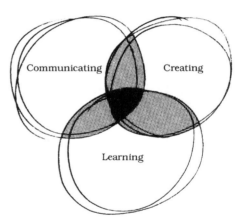

Graphic expression is used for all three processes—communicating, learning, and creating.

Communication

As we have noted, graphic symbols on maps enable the information on the map to be more easily understood. Similar kinds of graphically expressed symbols make other concepts easy to communicate. In fact, it is often much easier to communicate simple, concise concepts through graphic symbols than it is through written words. A picture often really is worth a thousand words!

Because the mind sees visual images and patterns, if you can create visual patterns on paper, you can learn and remember more easily. It's usually easier to remember an illustration in a book, for example, than it is to remember a written concept that you read in hundreds of pages of material.

An example of the use of graphic symbols is the blueprint for a building. Graphic symbols are used to help the architect conceive the idea for the structure of the building. The same graphic symbols are used to communicate to the contractor to turn the structure from paper into reality. And finally, the carpenter uses the blueprints as a guide to build the structure correctly and according to the architect's specifications.

Recollection

Have you ever gone someplace and later had someone ask you how to get there? You close your eyes and you think for a minute. You can see the destination in your mind's eye. You know exactly what it looks like but you just can't remember the exact route you took to get there. You may even have to hop in your car and start to drive to this destination to trigger your recall. As you pass the landmarks along the way the picture comes back in your mind and you remember again exactly where you are going and what route to take to the point that you can now create a map.

The mind has a tendency to learn and recall visually. Therefore, graphic expression is a way of extending the mind's ability to learn and remember more things.

Creativity

Graphic expression expands the creative potential of the mind. Thoughts are fleeting: they flash into the mind and then they disappear just as rapidly. Because creative thoughts are so fleeting, they don't seem to be real and are often lost. If you take those

same thoughts and put them on a piece of paper, they become real. You see them in detail and they remain. By capturing flashes of creative thoughts, much of the creative potential of the brain can be captured. If thoughts are not nailed down to a piece of paper, they are easily lost forever.

Also, because the mind thinks visually, a way to talk to the mind is by graphically refining thoughts. Graphically rendering the thoughts makes it easier to refine or change the thoughts so they become better and more concrete. This is done by graphically writing them down, not only in verbal forms but also in picture forms, symbols of what the mind is thinking.

Mastering Graphic Expression

There are three major steps in learning how to express your message graphically:

1. Choosing the appropriate symbol
2. Deciding the level of abstraction
3. Finding the essence of the concept that is to be graphically expressed

Choosing the Appropriate Symbol

The first step to improving graphic expression is to choose the appropriate symbols. Symbols are ways of expressing one's thoughts. Consider common symbols that depict a variety of concepts—poisonous materials, no smoking, exit, male or female, and so on. For every different concept there is a different kind of symbol to best express the concept. You must learn to choose appropriate symbols that convey what the concept is.

Because there are many different ways of expressing any thought, you must carefully choose the appropriate symbol that best expresses your thought by first determining the specific purpose on which to base the meaning of your symbol. If you want to express that something is deadly poisonous, then it is appropriate to use the skull and crossbones symbol. If you want to express a slightly different message for that same poisonous material—for example, that the material should be stored in closed bottles—you have changed the purpose of your symbol. This alteration to the message causes you to change the symbol—to graphically say something different. So the symbol is dependent upon your purpose.

In the following matrix of the eye there are many different points of view about that eye. Each one of those different illustrations on the bottom reveals a different point of view about the same subject matter: the eye. Notice that as the point of view changes, so does the graphic symbol that is used. This is what is meant by letting the point of view dictate the appropriate symbol.

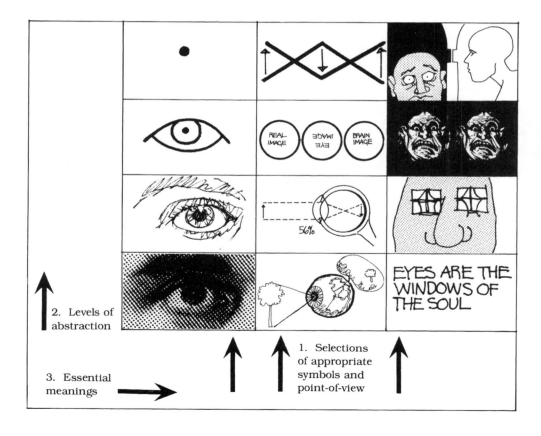

Deciding the Level of Abstraction

You must decide the level of abstraction for your symbol. What this means is that a symbol, to be effective, can be very realistic or very abstract. Sometimes it is more helpful to use a very realistic symbol, but other times it is better to choose an abstract symbol. Consider the matrix of the eye again. At the bottom left is a photo of a real human eye. You know exactly what it is. As you proceed upward in the matrix, the eye becomes sketchier until it becomes just a dot. That dot means "an eye" just as the photo does. If, for example, you were to use a photograph for an eye in a cartoon character, it would look out of place. It doesn't say any more about the character having an eye than does a single dot. And, in fact, the single dot is the more appropriate choice for the cartoon.

The same happens with other kinds of symbols. Sometimes symbols are too realistic, too complex. Simple, abstract symbols can serve well depending on the context.

Certain laws govern levels of abstraction. One is that the more abstract a symbol becomes, the more manageable it is. The symbol can be applied to a lot of different situations, although it can be more difficult to understand and more dependent upon its surroundings or its context to give that abstract symbol meaning. As in the eye matrix, that one single dot, which is an abstract symbol for an eye, could be used as an eye for a variety of cartoon characters. A more photographic eye, however, is more realistic, more concrete, but it is less manageable. It would fit on only one specific face and look good.

On the other hand, the more concrete or realistic in its application a symbol is, the more concrete and limited in its application is our understanding. You know more about the eye that is more carefully drawn or illustrated than you do about the dot. Concrete, realistic symbols are more understandable because they don't rely on outside situations or context to bring out the full meaning.

Finding the Essence

Graphic symbols have an essence of meaning. Once you find that essence of meaning it can become the basis for creating the graphic symbol. An example of finding the graphic symbol that carries the essence is shown in the flowers, crosses, and structures in the following image.

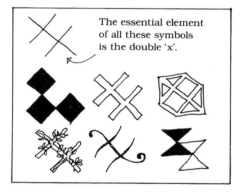

The essential element of all these symbols is the double 'x'.

All of these symbols have a similar pattern of a double cross laid at an angle. The graphic essence of expression in all of these symbols is the same—the double cross.

Look again at the eye matrix. The matrix shows how the eye functions. The top symbol of the Xs and arrows in the top center column is a graphic symbol depicting inversion. You strip it back to its essence, its meaning, and you discover than an X indicates "inversion." Once you get back to that basic symbol for inversion you could create some other illustrations that show inversion by using that same X as the underlying structure.

Creating Graphic Symbols

Now that you understand the principles of graphic expression, you are ready to see how it is done by creating your own symbol. Take the concept of a non-conformist. Begin by writing all of the things that a conformist is: regular, controlled, the same as someone else, and so on. A group of many people who are alike would be an example of conformity. Some visual examples of conformists or things that conform would be a group of business men in suits, ties, and coats, a school of fish all swimming in the

same way, a string of windows in a skyscraper that are exactly the same, a bunch of hippies all dressed alike, and so on.

By definition, a non-conformist is the opposite of a conformist. Now list all of the things that a non-conformist is: irregular, uncontrolled, different from other people, not a member of a group, and so on. A non-conformist is an individual rather than a member of a group.

Now that you have defined what a conformist is and a non-conformist is, you have stripped back the concept of a non-conformist to the essential meaning that is to be graphically symbolized.

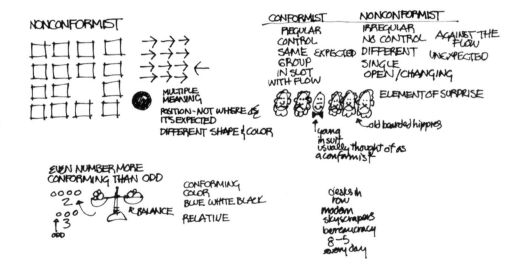

The visual examples of conformity—the monotonous skyscraper and the identical businessmen—can be modified to depict non-conformity as shown in these drawings of the skyscraper windows with one in which a person is peering out between the drapes and the identical businessmen walking in a line except one person dressed differently and walking in the other direction.

Consider the effective use of the element of surprise. You would normally expect that in the row of businessmen with a single non-conformist the non-conformist would be the hippie. But if you put hippies in a row and have one conservative businessman, then the conservative businessman becomes the (surprise!) non-conformist.

With practice you can create graphic symbols that effectively convey messages to your audience. As with anything you are not accustomed to doing, you may encounter some difficulty at first choosing and creating the appropriate symbol. Remember the following steps when creating your symbols to best communicate the concept or message that you wish to convey:

1. Let your determined point of view help dictate the appropriate symbol.

2. Determine the level of abstraction needed. If your symbol must be easily understood, choose a more realistic symbol. If your symbol must apply to many situations or have general application for a variety of symbols, then choose a more abstract symbol.

The finished drawing here used essential concepts to communicate nonconformity.
—One window in the building is done different from the rest.
—The texture of the window is different.
—The man below is going in a different direction.
—The dress of all the businessmen is the same, except for the lone man.
—The body size is different.
—The way of walking is different.

3. Find the essence of the concept in order to find the correct symbol. Strip back the concept to its basic meaning so that you can find a symbol to re-create the same meaning.

Exercises

It takes time and practice to develop your graphic expression skills, so work through the following exercises on your own.

Exercise 4.1

Match the following terms to the appropriate symbols from the images shown on the following page:

- Bell Telephone logo _____
- Poison _____
- United States of America _____
- Stop your car _____
- Fast _____
- Slow _____
- Look to the right _____
- Remove _____
- Half full _____
- Do not feed the bears _____
- Locked/unlocked _____
- Dollars _____
- Male _____
- Female _____
- North _____
- Ancient Indian symbol _____
- Clockwise _____
- Sign language _____
- Backpacking _____
- A hobo symbol meaning "a kind lady lives here" _____
- Fire prevention _____
- Sixteenth note _____
- Ranger station _____
- Resistor _____

Exercise 4.2

Make a grid similar to the eye matrix shown in this chapter for the other four senses:

- Hearing
- Smell
- Touch
- Taste

Exercise 4.3

Use these points of view to express characteristics:

- Visually express the *function* of the sense.
- Visually express the *form* of the sense.
- Visually express an *attribute* of the sense.

Exercise 4.4

Visually express five of the following sayings:

- Politics makes strange bedfellows.
- Taken with a grain of salt.
- It's not what it's all cracked up to be.
- Pay through the nose.
- March to the beat of a different drummer.
- The whole ball of wax.
- The show must go on.
- Paddle your own canoe.
- Out of the frying pan and into the fire.
- Leave no stone unturned.
- It's no skin off my nose.

Exercise 4.5

Visually illustrate two of the following concepts:

- Influential
- Polarity
- Obstinate
- Self-actualization
- Counter-culture
- Thinking
- Security
- Meaningless
- Reciprocity
- Recoil
- Oneness
- Sullen indifference

Exercise 4.6

Create a symbol for a sign to communicate three of the following concepts:

- Poison
- Don't open
- Hospital zone
- Unplug
- Sleeping permitted
- Camping permitted
- Turn left
- Must be accompanied by an adult
- Beware of undertow
- Live poisonous snake
- Wet paint
- Upside down
- Muggers beware
- Cold
- Elephant crossing
- Veterinarian
- Shoplifters will be arrested
- Don't sneeze
- Scratching allowed
- Don't feed the animals

Exercise 4.7

Draw a symbol that signifies three of the following sports or physical activities:

- Running
- Javelin throwing
- Discus
- Weight lifting
- Boxing
- Swimming
- Playing hop-scotch
- Jumping rope
- Playing marbles
- Hockey

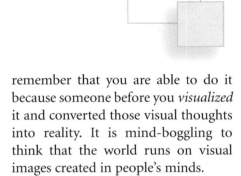

CHAPTER 5

GRAPHIC CREATION

I t's important—in fact, it is essential—that we become more visual. Our American society is dominated by verbal thinking. We learn alphabets, words, and numbers in school. Art and drawing are down played as somehow being less important. Yet everything—every machine, every invention, every modern convenience—existed first as a visual thought in someone's mind. Consider how important visual thinking really is. We owe our modern luxurious lifestyle to visual thinking. Doesn't it seem logical that we ought to learn to expand the creative visual potential inside all of us to foster our innovation and creativity?

The next time you watch TV, flip a light switch, or ride in an automobile

remember that you are able to do it because someone before you *visualized* it and converted those visual thoughts into reality. It is mind-boggling to think that the world runs on visual images created in people's minds.

In this chapter, you will learn:

- How to expand your creative potential through the expansion of your visual creativity.

- The role of using metaphors to form new ideas.

- How to apply methods for creative problem-solving individually and in group settings.

Ideas Don't Come from Nothing

There is no such thing as a creative idea that originates from nothing. Ideas come from the mind. A mind filled with knowledge, experiences, and an acute observation of the surrounding world is more likely to bring forth creative ideas.

One major problem with creative ideas is that because ideas are only thoughts in the beginning, they are easily lost. In order to "keep" those ideas, it's critical to commit them to a piece of paper. Once drawn or written down, the ideas are saved. Once on paper, the ideas can be evaluated properly, refined, and improved. Get your thoughts down on paper so you can develop them!

Imagination

The greatest source of ideas is the human mind. An artist tends to rely on his sensory organs—principally eyes and ears—to soak up impressions of life that are then stored in the mind. This bank of ideas can be recalled during the creative process whenever needed. When this memory is forti-fied with strong artistic skills, the out-flow of responses can be enhanced.

Learning to utilize this memory bank in a creative way is the greatest and most essential challenge in the development of your rapid visualization skills. You must develop the ability to tackle themes or subject matter with enthusiasm and confidence to enable your sketching to produce fruitful creative results. Remember that this kind of sketching—rapid visualization of ideas—trades accuracy and detail for expressiveness. The goal is not drawing to create a photo-accurate image; it is drawing sketchy, loose images that help you come up with or refine ideas. Idea drawing may be nothing more than lines that have meaning to you, but are meaningless to someone else looking at them. You may miss on the details but strike it rich on creative solutions. You can permit yourself to draw more spontaneously and even recklessly when necessary to encourage creativity.

Although at first you may feel wobbly in tackling a piece of white paper, after you get seriously involved in the process (usually after numerous efforts) the creative juices flow and you learn to trust both your memory and imagination. Drawings may be quite simple. Just working with abstract shapes and patterns may serve your purpose. You may even repeat a single subject idea in different fashions. The scribbles around the edge of your phone book or calendar reflect this type of improvised doodling.

The most important step is to begin practicing this imaginative sketching with pencil and paper. Allow your mind to work freely on a variety of subject matter.

Creative Ideas

Creative ideas are rarely new. In most cases, they are old concepts combined in a new and useful way to improve upon the original. For example, the electric toothbrush is just an electric motor and a toothbrush combined to improve upon the traditional toothbrush. Ben Franklin invented the first bifocal glasses by combining two lenses in one pair of glasses. The telephone is a combination of Alexander Graham Bell's knowledge of the human ear coupled with magnetism and electricity.

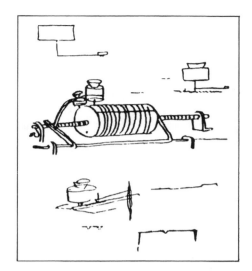

A sketch of a phonograph by Thomas Edison.

All creative ideas are logical connections. Sometimes these connections seem irrational or illogical to an outside observer, but they are logical connections to the originator of an idea. If someone said, for example, that marbles are very similar to oil, you might laugh. But if you envision lubricating oil as millions of tiny marbles sandwiched between two surfaces, you can see the logical similarity.

As this example demonstrates, making logical connections between objects is easier at abstract levels than at real levels. Physically, liquid oil is not like a solid glass marble, but if you understand that, abstractly, oil often behaves as tiny beads of fluid, then it is easy to make the logical connection.

The Vs illustrated in the following graphic visually explain how abstraction helps create logical relationships. A snail and a man have nothing in common at the concrete level depicted by the bottom of the V; however, as you compare them in more general, abstract terms, they have more in common.

Any object can be compared to any other object from an abstract point of view. Pick two objects and try comparing them to see for yourself. This abstraction method might prove to be one of the most productive idea development processes you could ever master.

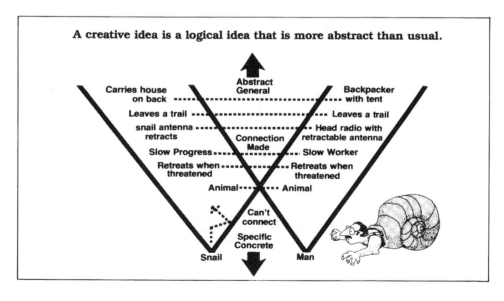

The Metaphor

Human beings need order in their lives. We seek an understandable framework on which to fasten new ideas and experiences. We understand the new by linking it with our knowledge of the past.

A metaphor is the comparison of the meaning and attributes of one thing to the meaning and attributes of something else.

For example:

> The Internet is an information superhighway.
>
> My boss is a pig.
>
> All the world is a stage.

Metaphors can seem absurd at first—until the relationship is clear. For example, on the surface the Internet may seem nothing like an actual superhighway made of concrete and speeding vehicles; however, when you look at a more abstract level to identify the relationship of vessels (information on the Internet and motor vehicles on the superhighway) traveling long distances at a high rate of speed you can begin to see the similarity.

To learn from a metaphor the learner must be an active participant. He must act and make some decision—take some risk. He does not manipulate, but invests something of himself so that growth may result.

After analyzing the data relevant to the structure of the atom, Lord Rutherford sought a model of the system he had discovered and found it in the solar system. Later experiments modified Rutherford's metaphor about the atom as a microscopic solar system, next using a metaphor of shells to understand the atom's structure. As knowledge advanced, the metaphor changed—scientists still needed some metaphor for comprehension—first the solar system, then shells, and who knows what next.

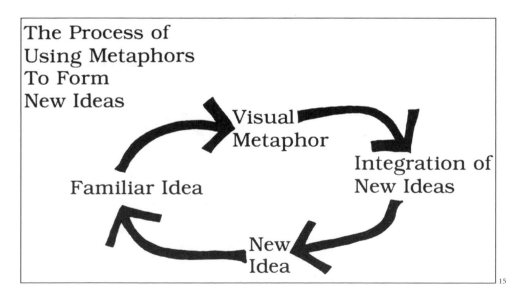

The Process of Using Metaphors To Form New Ideas

Visual Metaphor

Integration of New Ideas

Familiar Idea

New Idea

15

A metaphor often is used to describe the emotions by comparing them with the physical world. Shakespeare penned, "Shall I compare thee to a summer's day?" and Victor Hugo wrote, "Laughter is the sun that drives winter from the human face."

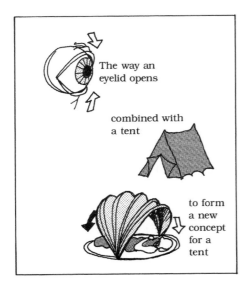

The way an eyelid opens

combined with a tent

to form a new concept for a tent

Metaphors are helpful in generating new meaning from old or unfamiliar concepts. Comparing the qualities of one thing to another creates new relationships. Visual metaphors are essential to many professions for the development of ideas. An architect, for example, must rely on visual metaphors to create new buildings. Just as Shakespeare used verbal metaphors to add life and give interest to his plays, visual metaphors are used by the architect to give life and interest to a building. Frank Lloyd Wright, considered by many to be the greatest architect of the 20th Century, used metaphors in the design of his unique buildings. Hallways would burst into the freedom and light of a spacious room, giving a feeling of security and warmth. Shapes and colors for buildings were patterned after shapes and colors found in nature. Room configurations were arranged to create certain feelings for the inhabitants of his buildings.

Collective Creativity for Groups or Individuals

Problem solving in a group can be especially productive. This kind of collective problem solving is often referred to as *brainstorming*. However, the creative methods that produce results when a group of people collectively brainstorm a problem also work well for individuals.

Creative solutions can be found by applying certain methods. If you can cause your mind to think in ways that produce creative new ideas, logically you will be more creative. Rapid visualization helps refine ideas. The brainstorming methods outlined in the remainder of this chapter produce creative results. Your ability to express these creative solutions in some visual form on paper is essential to the refining of the embryonic ideas. Use rapid visualization to express the ideas. It will be faster and easier than trying to verbalize many of the creative expressions.

Rules for Finding Creative Solutions

The following rules increase your ability to find creative solutions:

1. State the problem.

The development of new ideas usually comes when you have a problem—a need that must be met. Jonas Salk would not have developed the polio vaccine without the problem of an epidemic of people dying and being crippled by the disease. And before he could find the cure for polio, he had to determine what was causing the disease. He had to *identify* the problem before he could *solve* it.

Identify the real problem. Don't be misled by preconceived notions. For example, many people tried to solve the problem of cleaning dirty floors by improving the design of the broom. But only H.G. Booth realized that the problem was not poorly designed brooms—it was removing the dirt. Booth threw out the broom and invented the vacuum cleaner, which reversed wind to suck up dirt.

How a problem is stated exerts tremendous control over how it is solved. The definition of a problem can dictate a solution before creative thinking can begin. Be like H.G. Booth—don't confine yourself by trying to improve old methods that don't work well. Get to the *real* problem and forget the same old solutions that have been tried dozens of times before.

2. Pick a subject or problem that is understood by all involved.

A lot of time can be wasted if people in your group don't know the problem they are trying to solve. In a group setting, present all of the necessary background to the group.

3. Write out all ideas and objectives so everyone can see them.

In a group setting, use a chalkboard, overhead projector screen, or some other device to write out all ideas so everyone in the group can see them. If you are working alone, don't think you can get away without putting the random thoughts on paper. One of the key secrets to successful brainstorming is having all of the thoughts

down on paper. Thoughts that seem crazy at first can yield extremely effective solutions when combined with other seemingly crazy thoughts. If all thoughts are not written down in the first place, you will not have the opportunity to combine them to get the final perfect solution. Use words, phrases, or pictures—anything that rapidly will capture the essence of the ideas as they flow from the individuals in the group. New and different relationships between the ideas expressed will cause additional ideas, but only if all the ideas can be seen together.

4. Concentrate on quantity not quality.

A great scientist once said, "The way to get a good idea is to have lots of ideas." Produce as many ideas as possible so you will have more to pick from at the end of the brainstorming session. After the session, it is easy to eliminate useless, ridiculous, or impossible ideas; however, it is extremely difficult to find quality in a short list of ideas. Without *quantity*, you'll most likely miss the *quality* ideas too.

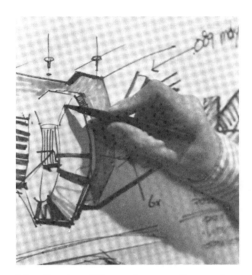

Visualization skills can increase the number of ideas you have and can improve their quality.

5. Keep it loose.

Nothing can stop effective, creative brainstorming faster than a leader with a Napoleon complex—someone who commands others to perform by attempting to *force* others to produce good ideas. Keep unnecessary structure out of the process. The command "Give me good ideas!" will do just the opposite by inhibiting the group's cre-ativity and thoughts. Brainstorming requires an open and free environment that gives an incentive for idea protection.

6. Hitchhike.

Let each participant's thoughts build upon another's ideas. Sometimes ideas that initially are off-beat and impractical will trigger other ideas that can be quite useful. That ridiculous idea that you don't want to say out loud could prompt someone else to think of the perfect solution.

In brainstorming, don't narrow your vision. Search all over in your experiences for ideas that relate to the problem. You may find an idea in literature, yesterday's breakfast, or an insect's mating habits. Connect ideas that don't seem to belong together, and they may inspire the perfect solution.

The essence of getting good ideas is forming meaningful connections between knowledge and experiences in our lives. What would modern physics be like if Isaac Newton had not recognized the connection between a falling apple and the bodies in the heavens? Where would modern medicine be without William Harvey making a connection between the function of a pump and the working of a human heart? How is a sunrise like hope, a cockroach like a tank, or a tree like a young boy? As teacher and artist Gyorgy Kepes said, "The separa-tion of our sensual, emotion, and rational faculties into separate little slots is the prime reason for the form-less nature of our environment and the lives we live."

7. No "no-no"s.

Your goal is ideas, not judgments. By letting your mind run wild you can eliminate mental blocks to creative solutions. Don't judge what you or anyone else may think. If you have an idea, don't hesitate for fear of being judged. Don't squelch someone else's seemingly dumb idea either. It may inhibit that person from participat-ing, and you need everyone's input in the process. Evaluate the ideas gener-ated *after*, not during, the brainstorm-ing session.

8. Last is best.

Often the last half of a brainstorming session generates the best ideas. It takes the first half of the session to warm up and get all of the usual responses and habitual solutions out of the way. When these are out, the new ideas and creative solutions tend to appear. Unfortunately, most brainstorming sessions end too soon, having generated nothing more than the old mental clichés instead of new ideas.

I do not know any truly creative person that could store creative new thoughts in his or her mind. Great innovators throughout history have recorded their ideas in some form or another—most often in visual form. If you study the notes of great creative minds like Albert Einstein, Leonardo DaVinci, Issac Newton, Alexander Graham Bell, Thomas Edison, and others, you find their notes are rich with visual images. They didn't just *write* their thoughts, they *visually sketched* their thoughts. If you want to be creative, you need to capture your thoughts. A visual sketch of the thought can often be much more expressive than words used to describe the thought.

If you do not capture creative thoughts as they come to you, they will come and go like the wind. Great creative thinkers of the past probably are no more creative than you are, but they put their thoughts down on paper for all to see. If you record your thoughts on paper, you will probably be amazed at how creative you really are. Creative thoughts are nothing if they are not recorded. Resolve to begin sketching your thoughts today. You will be delighted at the creative expanse your mind possesses.

Exercises

Following are some visual exercises to improve creative potential. They are designed to get ideas flowing and enable you to learn how to capture the thoughts before they float away never to be seen again.

Exercise 5.1

Illustrate any four of the words in the following list:

- Hot dog
- Chairman
- Warfare
- Eastern
- Inhuman
- Flippant
- Headlong
- Rubber band
- Defiance
- Dispute
- Antidote
- Pigment
- Vengeance
- Tangle
- Usurp
- Fallacy
- Tissue
- Tempestuous
- Hollow
- Safeguard
- Winsome
- Underwear

Exercise 5.2

Combine an item from Column 1 with three items from Column 2 to make a new product.

Column 1

- Grapes
- Apple
- Orange
- Watermelon
- Corn on the cob
- Peas
- Tomatoes
- Rhubarb
- Carrot
- Bell pepper
- Walnut
- Celery
- Lettuce
- String bean

Column 2

- Apartment complex
- Drawers
- Jewelry
- Computer terminal
- Fountain
- Telephone
- Protective helmet
- Clothing
- Casegoods
- Light fixture
- Shoes
- Air transportation
- Water transportation
- Land transportation

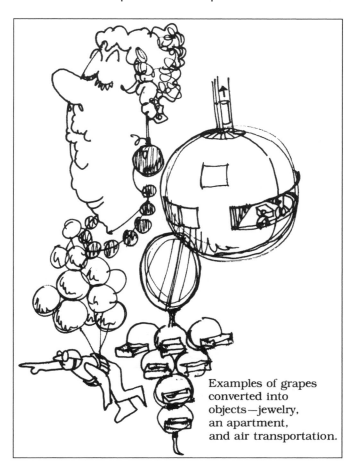

Examples of grapes converted into objects—jewelry, an apartment, and air transportation.

Exercise 5.3

Use your imagination to create five new senses for humans. In addition to sight, taste, hearing, smelling, and touch, you now have a new sense. Illustrate that sense and explain what the sense is.

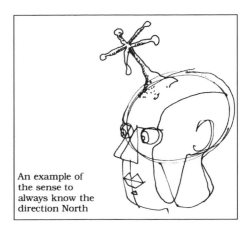

An example of the sense to always know the direction North

Exercise 5.4

Create five inventions that will enhance one of the existing senses.

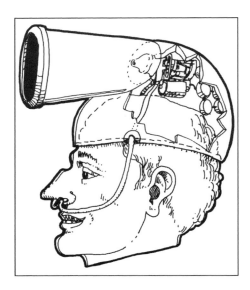

Exercise 5.5

Illustrate 10 new inventions that will be in use in the year 2050.

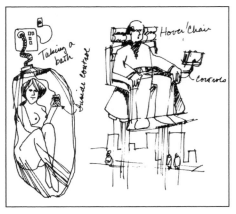

Exercise 5.6

Cut and paste items from magazines to create two new inventions. The inventions can be as realistic and useful (or as wild and outlandish) as you want them to be.

Exercise 5.7

Design a musical instrument to be played by one of the following life-forms.

- Octopus
- Gerbil
- Flea
- Worm
- Bird
- Bee
- Ant
- Giraffe
- Bat
- Alligator

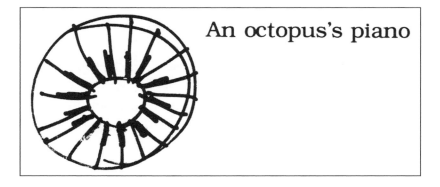

An octopus's piano

Exercise 5.8

The doodles on the next page combine to form what I call a "throw-up sheet". This sheet is an example of a catchall for the many ideas that emerged from my mind when given the assignment to create something. I find it fun to periodically create a new throw-up sheet for some wild idea just to keep my creative thinking powers sharpened.

Create your own throw-up sheet that contains any one of the concepts from the following list. Fill up the entire sheet with your ideas for this one thing you choose from the list.

- Better ways to carry clothes
- Better kinds of clothes
- Ways not to need any clothes
- Better ways to get information
- Directional lights
- Portable eating units
- One-person transportation vehicles
- One-person housing ideas
- Ways to grow food
- Things that expand and contract depending on the amount of light exposed
- Things that use camouflage

Exercise 5.9

Repeat Exercise 5.8, but do it with a group of people rather than alone.

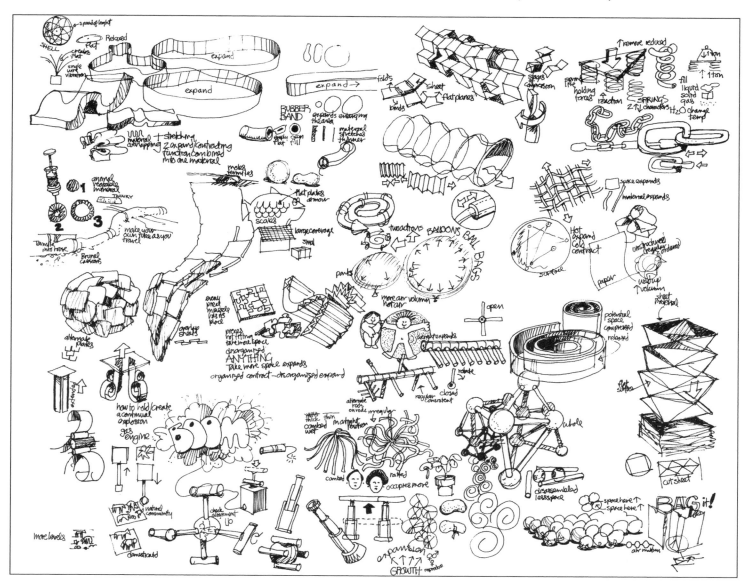

Exercise 5.10

Take material or technology from one discipline and apply it elsewhere. The following example depicts a new form of lighting created by combining light fixtures with pipe. For this exercise, combine any two of the following materials and applications you like to create your new invention.

- Plastic pipe
- 50 gallon drums
- Conduit
- Cement blocks
- Scaffolding
- Old tires
- Cable
- Rocks

- Lighting
- Moveable shelters
- Outdoor furniture
- Moveable exhibit
- Playground equipment
- Planter boxes
- Exercise equipment
- Bedroom furniture

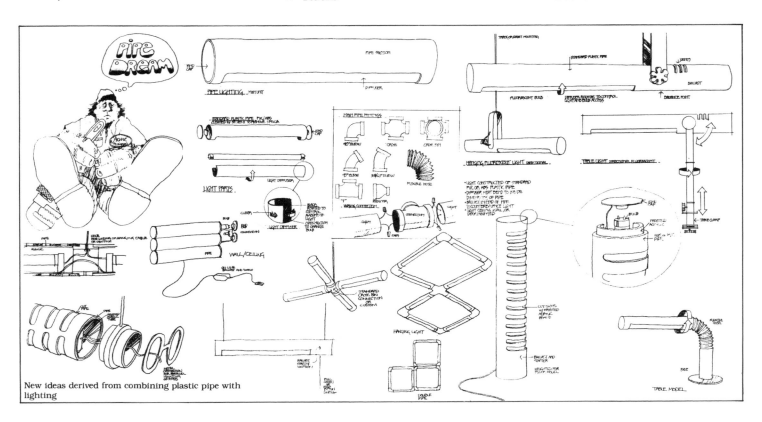

New ideas derived from combining plastic pipe with lighting

Exercise 5.11

Pick two items from the following list and illustrate how you will improve them for use in the future.

- Blimps
- Modular housing
- Emergency housing
- Maximum land utilization
- Crop growing systems
- Underwater vehicles
- Business offices
- Home recreation
- Clothing

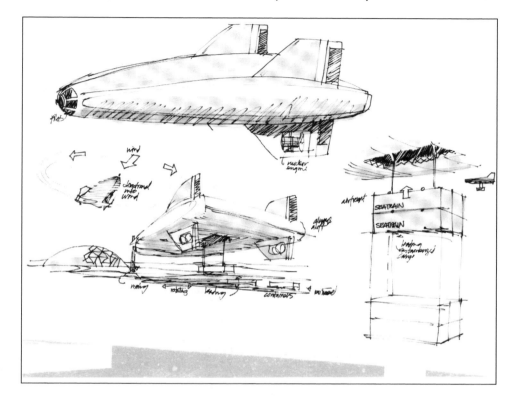

Exercise 5.12

You have just traveled to a newly discovered planet. You want to illustrate
for your friends back home what you
have seen and learned about the
inhabitants of this new planet.
Illustrate three of the following items.

- A species of wildlife
- A musical instrument
- A typical dwelling
- Scenes from the latest box
  office hit
- A favorite recreational pastime
- The national flag
- A common medical procedure
- A favorite meal

A Grupla holding the national flag

The winning float in the Grupla Winter Festival

CHAPTER 6

LEARNING WITH VISUALS

V isuals can be a great aid to learning, understanding, and remembering. As the saying goes, a picture is worth a thousand words. It is easier to see and understand than to hear and process information. Visuals can increase your ability to learn something.

In this chapter, you will learn:

- Why visuals aid learning and comprehension.
- How to take visual notes.
- How to use Rapid Viz techniques for your own learning or for teaching others.

A visual explanation of the Doppler Effect.

The following story of one of my students illustrates how visual learning can increase comprehension and retention of information.

Mary was a student in one of my classes. She wasn't an outstanding student; she was an average student, but she worked hard and performed well in her art and design classes. One day she was feeling discouraged and confided in me that she was not doing well in a psychology class. She explained that she just couldn't grasp the total concepts. She was disappointed to be earning a C in the class. She didn't want an average grade—she wanted an A or B. I suggested that she try taking visual notes rather than verbal notes. I explained that by structuring things with visual patterns, geometric shapes, or doodle-type drawings she may be able to understand and remember the subject more easily. After a thorough explanation of the technique Mary caught on and agreed to try it for herself.

At the end of that semester Mary came to me to proudly announce that she had earned an A in her psychology class as the result of visual note-taking. She said that drawing out in visual patterns made it much easier for her to understand then later recall what she had learned in class. Mary's story is just one of many similar situations that I encountered while teaching.

Another example of the success of visual note-taking is Evelyn Wood, nationally recognized teacher of speed reading. If you have ever observed an Evelyn Wood demonstration, you have seen students rapidly reading many pages in a book and then recalling in detail what they read. Her students use a visual note-taking technique to remember what they read in books. Teaching students to read rapidly is only a part of Evelyn Wood's genius. I think the greatest skill that Evelyn Wood teaches these students is the ability to remember what they read. The way she does this is by teaching visual note-taking and recall to help students learn faster.

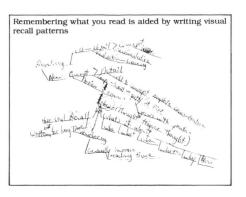

Remembering what you read is aided by writing visual recall patterns

Visuals Aid Understanding

The strength of visuals to aid understanding is threefold:

- Visuals create a "big picture" to simplify complex concepts.
- Visuals provide structure of concepts in the mind's eye.
- Visuals form strong mental images for the mind to recall.

Visuals enable you to see a whole picture at a glance rather than just the small, individual parts. By seeing the whole structure, you can see the relationship of each of the parts. This whole structure and the relationship of the parts lead your mind to the details of the concept that you are trying to understand. By showing the whole and the relative parts at a glance, visuals make complex concepts easier to understand.

The following illustration is a visual of a complex concept—weather conditions on earth resulting from heat gain and loss from solar/earth interaction. The illustration provides an overall view of how the system works, and by understanding the overall system, it is then easier to understand the details in perspective as you learn more about the concept. Once you have a visual image of the system's pattern, if I talk about the importance of solar energy to life—how solar energy affects the weather and atmospheric conditions on earth—that makes sense because you can see how that happens. The details are easy to understand because you have seen the whole picture.

Another thing that visuals do is give structure to things. It is a human tendency to seek order. We want to have an orderly life. We want things to make sense. We want things to relate to something else. If something just seems to come out of nowhere or if we hear things that don't make sense,

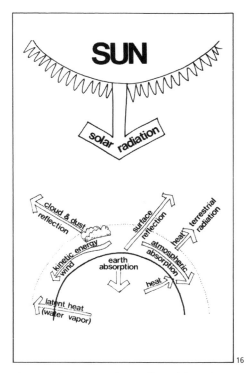

16

The weather on Earth as affected by solar radiation.

it is uncomfortable to us. Visual patterns are one way to help things to make sense. They form a picture of the relationship of parts. By relating things one to another we make sense out of things. So visual patterns feed our natural tendency to seek order; they help give order to the things that we learn.

Complex things are made easy to understand by tying the concept to a visual pattern. Structures give order to details. When we see the whole pattern of something, then it is easy to understand the parts. It is easy to understand the details if we see the relationship of the parts. Visuals help complex things seem easy to understand.

A third way visual notes help is that the mind seeks strong mental images to recall. Visual notes are a strong mental image created for the mind to recall. This image makes it easier for the mind to picture what is happening and remember what is happening.

How To Take Visual Notes

Visual note-taking is relatively simple as long as you do a couple of basic things. First, you must develop some kind of structure for your note-taking. With this structure, you can tie the parts and the details together so that everything will make sense to you later to aid your recall. To develop your structure, begin by identifying the central theme of the subject matter. Once you've identified the central theme, sort out the different elements that apply to it—the stories, the facts, the figures, the different details. Ask yourself the key questions: Who? What? When? Where? Why? How? The answers to these questions form a structure for understanding the concept. Put these elements around the central theme to form a relationship. This process is demonstrated in the following example of visual note-taking on the body's physical responses to fear.

In this example, the central theme is fear. As you look at the elements of the visual note, you can readily identify the various elements related to the body's physical reaction to fear—the pupils dilate, blood pressure increases, adrenaline is released, the hair stands on end, and so on. The visual enables you to better recall these reactions that occur throughout the body and where they occur in the body.

As you can see in this example, we have drawn a fairly complex body; however, you could do the same thing with a very simple, stick figure drawing as well.

The next example of visual note-taking was created to demonstrate the measurement of time using natural means.

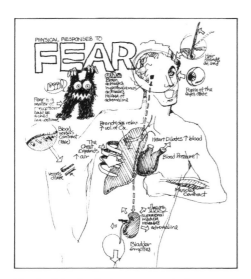

The body's physical responses to fear.

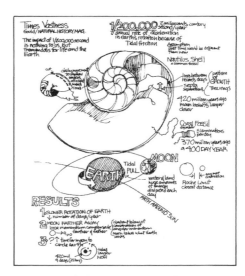

How natural phenomena record the passing of time.

The third example is a simplified visual pattern that demonstrates the need for education to include balanced learning in both scientific and artistic fields. Even though the majority of the information is written out, the inclusion of the circles and hands makes a visual image for the mind to remember to aid recall of the written out information.

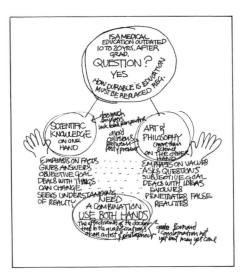

Education should include balanced learning.

Mark Twain—A Visual Note-Taking Pioneer

On occasion you may find yourself responsible for making a speech at a professional conference, convention, testimonial dinner, whatever. Studies have shown that people rank public speaking as their number one fear, while death is number two. Amazing!

One way to overcome the fear of public speaking is to improve your speaking skills. You may be surprised to find how effectively visual note-taking can aid in the development of your public speaking skills.

Most of us wish we could speak eloquently and easily with the words flowing naturally, sprinkled with the perfect anecdotes and humor and backed by a clear grasp of the facts and detail. That's the way good speakers come across. And those good speakers don't speak from notes, so how do they do it?

Mark Twain faced these same problems.[17] He wasn't a particularly skillful speaker at first, but he became one of the most successful orators in American history through the use of visual note-taking techniques. Twain worked out his own system through trial and error throughout his lifetime, and his system wasn't revealed until years after his death when a post-mortem essay was published. The system Twain developed was so effective for him that he claimed he could remember an entire speech 25 years after he gave it and could recall it in complete detail through a single act of recall.

In his early days as a lecturer, Twain used the usual full pages of text notes to keep his thoughts in order. He'd write down the beginnings of key sentences to take him from one point to another. Typically he would write and memorize 11 key sentence beginnings for a lecture. The problem was it just didn't work. He'd remember the sentence but forget the appropriate order causing him to stop and consult his notes, which spoiled the flow and spontaneity of the entire speech.

His next attempt was to not only memorize the key sentences but also the first letter of each sentence to keep them in order. That didn't work either—not even when he limited the number of key sentences to 10 and inked the first letter of each on his fingers!

"I kept track of the fingers for awhile," Twain wrote, "then I lost it, and after that I was never quite sure which finger I'd used last."

Twain even tried licking off the inked letters as he went along with his speech, but found that people would notice he was more interested in his fingers than his subject. Inevitably a listener or two would approach him afterward to ask what was wrong with his hands.

Then came the realization—the great turning point—that it was difficult to visualize letters, words and sentences, but pictures are easy to recall. Images grab you—especially if you draw them yourself.

"In two minutes I made six pictures with a pen," Twain reported. "They did the work of 11 catch-sentences, and did it perfectly."

Twain was no artist, but he did the drawings anyway. Samples of his artwork indicate crude drawings—not really considered art, but they did the job. Having drawn the pictures himself, he found that he could throw them away and still recall the images at will. (Try it yourself. You will be surprised how effective it is.)

Samples of his visual note-taking include a haystack with a wiggly line under it to represent a rattlesnake to remind him to talk about ranch life in the West. Slanting lines with an umbrella under them and the Roman numeral II referred to a great wind that would strike Carson City every afternoon at 2 o'clock. A couple of jagged lines representing lightning reminded him to move on to the subject of weather in San Francisco where he noted there wasn't any lightning or thunder.

Twain's visual note-taking system was so effective in preparing him for lectures that he spoke without text notes from that day forward and his system never failed him. Before each lecture or pubic appearance, he drew a picture for each section of his speech, all strung out in a row like a storyboard. He would look at the images when he was finished and then destroy them. When he spoke, the images were again fresh and sharp in his mind. If he wanted to add comments based on the remarks of a previous speaker or presenter, he simply created and inserted another picture in his series of images.

Why Visuals Work

Twain was a writer, so it may be surprising to you that writing down his thoughts didn't work for him. It was much easier and more effective for him to recall the visual patterns he created, and the same is true for nearly everyone. There are several simple reasons why visuals create such strong mental images:

- Visuals form a unique mental image.
- Visuals provide a general overview.
- Visuals simplify concepts.
- Visuals create mental order.

Forming a Unique Mental Image

It is naturally easier for the mind to recall visuals as they create a unique mental image. If you look at words on a page, you see a gray pattern. If you look at a visual picture, more often than not the picture is much different than any other visual picture you see. The image is unique. This creates a mental image for the mind and that image is easy to recall.

Providing a General Overview

Another advantage of visual pictures is that they provide a general overview. Visuals are a help because they take the mind from general to specific. Concepts are more easily understood and remembered when they are taken from general to specific.

Simplifying Concepts

Visuals simplify concepts that would otherwise seem complex or intimidating. By viewing a key concept as simplified by a visual drawing, it becomes easier to understand the details related to the concept.

Creating Mental Order

Visuals aid in recall because they create mental order that all individuals need. Humans naturally want things to make sense and have order. Visuals are an easy way to give order and sense to concepts.

The Importance of Your Own Visuals

Visuals help you remember things best when you create those visuals yourself. Your drawings don't need to be fancy or even particularly artistic; they only need to be a visual pattern that makes sense to you. If you create the pattern, no matter what that pattern is, it is better than if you rely on someone else's pattern to help your mind recall the concept.

If you are familiar with the term *mnemonics*, you can see parallels in the way these techniques work. Mnemonics is the technique of using related sounds to trigger the memory. For example, I had a friend that could not remember the name Arlene Cook, so he created his own mental image of an alligator that was leaning against a wall. This alligator wore a chef's hat to trigger the association with "cook". Once he created this mental image through the combined use of mnemonics and visualization, he no longer had trouble remembering the name Arlene Cook.

The methods for creating visual memory patterns are the same as the ones used for creating visual note-taking patterns. You begin with the central theme behind the concept, identify the related supportive elements to that theme, and then create the structure of your visual. No matter how strange the visual pattern—even as odd as an alligator leaning against a wall wearing a chef's hat—the structure you create relates the parts to the central theme. As you see in the examples found throughout this book, visual memory patterns take a variety of shapes, sizes, and styles—whatever is necessary to create a visual pattern to aid you with recall of memory.

Draw, in your own style, whatever reminds you of the story or topic. For example, sales must increase could be drawn with a vertically pointed arrow and a dollar sign. If you have figures to remember, draw them coming out of people's mouths, in pyramids, under a building, whatever will trigger the image and the numbers in your memory. Often the wilder the image, the easier it will be to remember.

Rapid Viz Aids Learning and Recall

Most people readily recognize the value of visual aids. They look at and remember visuals they encounter in books such as diagrams that communicate concepts. However, most people do not draw their own visuals to aid understanding. If you employ the Rapid Viz note-taking technique, your ability to learn and recall will be increased greatly.

Exercises

Exercise 6.1

Visually depict at least five of the following concepts:

- Characterization
- Entropy
- Euphemism
- Structural stability
- Harmony
- Network
- Linear induction
- Synergy
- Arms race
- Balanced budget
- Injection molding
- Platonic love
- Deductive reasoning
- Ecosystem
- Heat pump
- General system theory
- Microeconomics
- Transactional analysis
- Offset printing
- Carbuncle
- Sterling engine
- Meiosis
- Learning curve
- Specialty advertising
- Checks and balances
- Soliloquies
- Manifold
- Legume

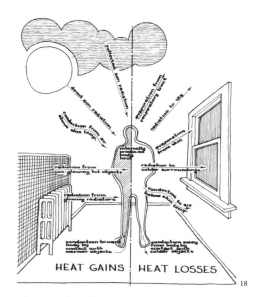

The transfer of heat.

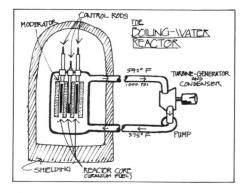

The boiling-water reactor.

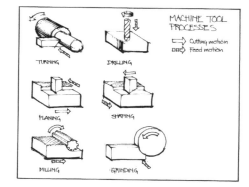

Basic machining processes.

Exercise 6.2

Visually depict how to do any three of the following activities:

- Make bread
- Start a car
- Eat an apple
- Cut grass
- Swing dance
- Evoke a response
- Follow a scent
- Cut your own hair
- Sell a wristwatch
- Make money
- Tie a shoelace
- Pick a nose
- Change a tire
- Install a lock
- Drill a well
- Write a poem
- Destroy a tank
- Play soccer

Exercise 6.3

Watch an informational movie or TV show. Be aware of the different visual explanations given to communicate the intended message. Take notes using the visual note-taking technique. Later rethink the movie or show by comparing the use of visuals used to your choices for visual note-taking. Compare your visual notes with another source (an encyclopedia or online references) that explains the same subject matter and record an assessment of your notes.

_____

_____

_____

_____

Exercise 6.4

Read two magazine articles. Take visual notes of what you read. Revisit your notes two or three weeks later to test your recall of the articles. Then reread the articles. Objectively critique how effectively and accurately your visual notes aided your recall of the content of the articles.

Magazine Article 1:

_____

_____

_____

_____

Magazine Article 2:

_____

_____

_____

_____

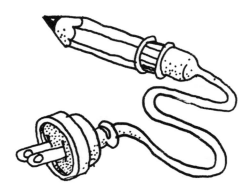

APPENDIX A

ADDITIONAL EXERCISES

This appendix contains additional exercises for your own personal study or for use in a classroom environment. These exercises are meant to challenge your new skills and strengthen your visualization and graphic expression techniques.

Exercise A.1

Learning to visualize can be achieved by causing your mind to see new views of objects. Draw a three-dimensional sectional view of the object described by the front, top, and side views of the objects shown on the next page. (Hint: The section views are as though a portion of the object were cut away.)

First Example

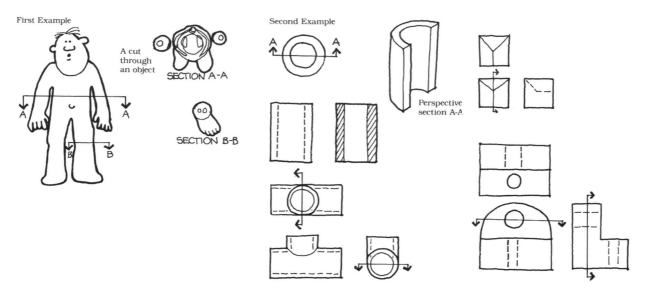

A cut through an object

SECTION A-A

SECTION B-B

Second Example

Perspective section A-A

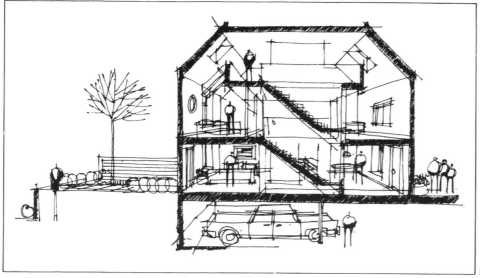

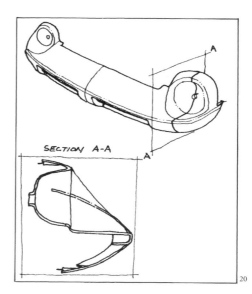

SECTION A-A

Exercise A.2

A key component of visualization is to see the internal workings of objects. The images shown on this page are examples of two techniques used to see internal views of objects. The van is shown as though the outer shell were transparent allowing you to see the internal parts. The hair dryer is shown as an exploded view of all of the internal parts.

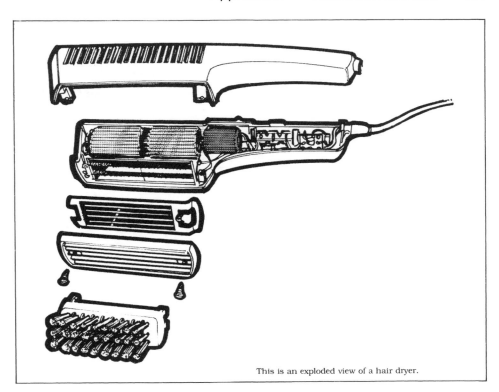

This is an exploded view of a hair dryer.

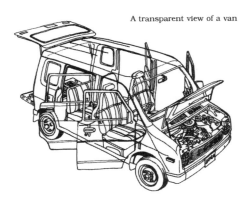

A transparent view of a van

Find a small gadget or appliance that you can disassemble. Take it apart and draw the parts using either of the two techniques shown—the transparent view or the exploded view.

Exercise A.3

Design five different styles of flash-light using the critical elements (light, switch, batteries, connection) shown in the following image.

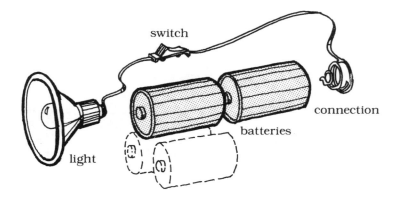

Exercise A.4

The two images on this page show real and imagined views of playground equipment. Create your own drawing of playground equipment that you would like to see built.

21

Exercise A.5

The photograph on the next page is of a narrow street that could be converted into something fabulous. Place a piece of tracing paper over the photograph to trace the structures. Now use that template to create a new "something" for the narrow street. It could be anything from a dog park to a pedestrian rest area to an outdoor café—whatever your mind can imagine.

Exercise A.6

Transform this old house into a new structure. The new building need not, and probably should not, appear anything like the original house. Improve it in any way you can imagine. (This technique of transforming something old into something new can be a source for numerous other exercises on your own.)

Exercise A.7

Grid sheets are visual comparisons of two variables. Grid sheets that analyze the different characteristics of a given situation can expand the visual mind. Study the following example to see how the grid pattern was used to analyze the problem. In this example, the dots on the chart indicate where the items listed across the top correspond to the items listed down the right side.

Select two variables you can compare to create your own grid. For example, create a grid depicting the number of people that walk along five different streets during different hours of the day. List one variable horizontally across the top or bottom and list the other variable vertically along the left edge of the grid. In this case, the two variables are the streets and the hours of the day.

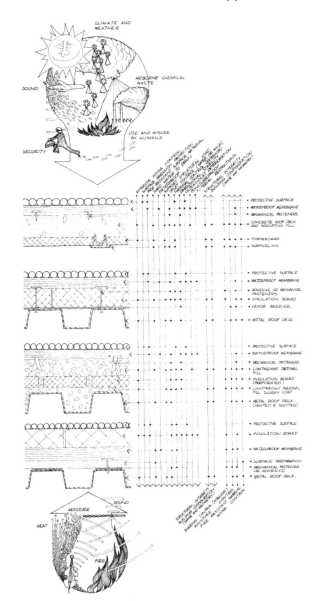

Exercise A.8

Creating new objects from simple shapes expands visual powers. The circular restaurant in the following image was created by combining cylindrical shapes. Use this technique to combine spherical or triangular shapes to create a new bank. If you wish to go further, combine other basic shapes to create new clothing apparel, new transportation equipment, or any other item you can imagine.

Exercise A.9

Create three drawings of ways the street in the following photograph could be improved or changed.

Exercise A.10

Draw three different design ideas for improving or changing the camper shown in this photo. Your drawings may include aesthetic or functional improvements to the camper. Use tracing paper to help you quickly draw the basic parameters of the camper, if necessary.

Exercise A.11

Flip visuals are a popular rapid visualization tool. Begin by drawing your own step-by-step cartoon show. When your drawings are completed, place them stacked from beginning to end on top of each other and flip through the drawings as you would flip through pages in a book to see your drawings in action.

Exercise A.12

Use tracing paper to copy the basic structure for this new electric automobile. Draw five different outer shells for the vehicle. Make each concept car as different and visually exciting as you can possibly imagine.

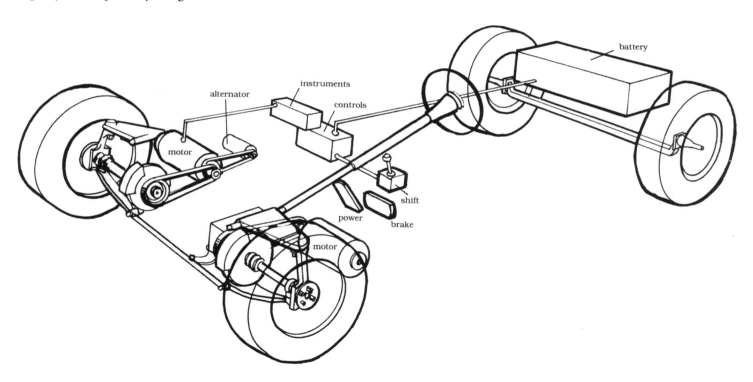

Exercise A.13

Create a power hand tool that does not need electricity as a power source. Your tool can be a redesign of an existing electric tool in use today or something completely new. Possible alternative power sources might include water, wind, gravity, light, geo-thermal, fly wheels, etc.

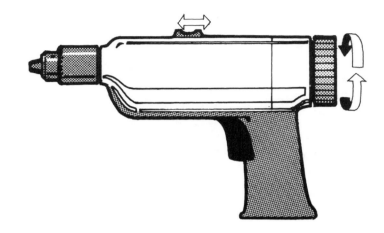

Exercise A.14

Imagine that a "matter transporter" has recently been invented. This device can transport matter from one location to another instantaneously. Distance is no problem.

List 25 positive results and 25 negative results from the invention of the matter transporter.

Illustrate three positive and three negative results that you listed.

25 Positive Results:

_____

_____

_____

_____

_____

_____

_____

_____

_____

_____

_____

_____

_____

_____

_____

_____

_____

_____

_____

_____

_____

_____

_____

25 Negative Results:

_____

_____

_____

_____

_____

_____

_____

_____

_____

_____

_____

_____

_____

_____

_____

_____

_____

_____

_____

_____

_____

_____

_____

Exercise A.15

Study the following sequence illustrations. Duplicate this sequential technique to create a seven sequence illustration of the following activities:

- Your drive to school or work
- A walk through a building
- A walk through a park
- A walk down your street
- A recent trip you took
- A visit to the grocery store

22

APPENDIX B

SUGGESTED READINGS

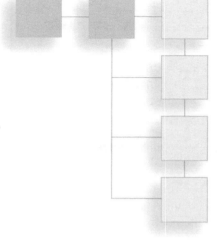

The following list includes some of the best books written by authors with years of experience in drawing, visualization, teaching, and developing visualization processes. Please take the time to find and read them all. I am sure you will find them to be helpful in your mastery of visualization, and valuable additions to your reference shelf.

Archigram, ISBN: 1568981945, Princeton Architectural Press.

Architectural Delineation, Earnest E. Burden, ISBN: 0070089396, McGraw-Hill.

Architectural Illustration: The Value Delineation Process, Paul Stevenson Oles, ISBN: 0442262744, Van Nostrand Reinhold Publishing Co.

Architectural Rendering: The Techniques of Contemporary Presentation, Albert O. Halse, ISBN: 0070256284, Mc-Graw Hill.

Design Drawing 2000 Edition, William Kirby Lockard, ISBN: 0393730409, W.W. Norton & Company.

Design Drawing Experiences 2000 Edition, William Kirby Lockard, ISBN: 0393730417, W.W. Norton & Company.

Design with Nature, Ian L. McHarg, ISBN: 047111460X, Wiley Pubishing.

Design Yourself!, Hanks and Belliston, ISBN: 1560520469, Crisp Learning.

Designers Dictionary, Bruce T. Barber, ASIN: B0006W43CS, Upson Company.

Designers Dictionary Two, Bruce T. Barber, ISBN: 091138054X, St. Books.

Draw! A Visual Approach to Thinking, Learning, and Communicating, Hanks and Belliston, ISBN: 0913232459, Crisp Learning.

Drawing the Head and Figure, Jack Hamm, ISBN: 0399507914, Perigee Books.

Drawing As a Means to Architecture, William Kirby Lockard, ISBN: 1560522232, Crisp Learning.

Drawings by American Architects, Alfred M. Kemper (editor), ISBN: 0471013692, John Wiley & Sons.

Experiences in Visual Thinking, Robert H. McKim, ISBN: 0818504110, Brooks/Cole Publishing Co.

Graphic Design for the Computer Age: Visual Communication for All Media, Edward A. Hamilton, ISBN: 0442113749, Van Nostrand Reinhold Publishing Co..

Graphic Problem-Solving for Architects and Builders, Paul Laseau, ISBN: 084360154X, Cahners Books.

How to Draw Animals, Jack Hamm, ISBN: 0399508023, Perigee Books.

Language of Drawing, Edward Hill, ASIN: B0006BOU40, Prentice-Hall.

Pencil Broadsides, Theodore Kautzky, ISBN: 0442110413, Van Nostrand Reinhold Publishing Co.

Perspective: A New System for Designers, Jay Doblin, ASIN: B0007DQJUA, Whitney Library of Design.

Perspective Drawing Handbook, Joseph D'Amelio, ISBN: 0486432084, Dover Publications.

The Big Yellow Drawing Book, Dan O'Neill, H.D. O'Neill, and Marian O'Neill, ISBN: 0967591902, Hugh O'Neill and Associates.

The Natural Way to Draw, Kimon Nicolaides, ISBN: 0395530075, Houghton Mifflin Co.

The New Drawing on the Right Side of Your Brain, Betty Edwards, ISBN: 0874774241, Tarcher Publishing.

The Pencil, Paul Calle, ISBN: 0823039900, Watson-Guptill Publications.

The Thames and Hudson Manual of Rendering with Pen and Ink, Robert W. Gill, ISBN: 0500680264, W.W. Norton & Co.

Visual Thinking, Rudolf Arnheim, ISBN: 0520242262, University of California Press.

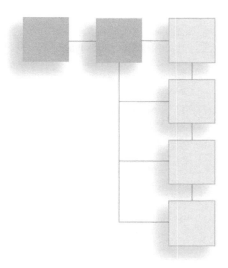

CREDITS

The following illustration and information sources were used in the creation of this book.

1. U.S. Steel Corporation

2. Droodle Book Series, Roger Price, Price-Stern Publisher

3. Abstracta Systems, Inc.

4. John M. Johansen and Associates, by Ashoik M. Bhavnani, New York, NY

5. From the paper "Design Approaches to the Fibrous Glass Reinforced Polyester Bathroom as Related to Market Needs" by David D. Tompkins and Merritt W. Seymour, Owens Corning Fiberglass Corporation

6. Drawing by Carl Landow, Manhattan Community College, Caudill Rowlett Scott

7. Drawing by Howard F. Elkus, AIA Headquarters Building, The Architects Collaborative

8. Drawing by John M. Johansen, Leap Frog Housing, John M. Johansen and Associates

9. Reprinted from the January 1977 issue of *Progressive Architecture*, copyright 1977, Reinhold Publishing Company, p. 73 (Richard Ridley and Associates)

10. *Symbol Sourcebook*, Henry Dreyfuss, McGraw-Hill Publishing Company

11. *Introduction to Engineering Design and Graphics*, George C. Blakley and Ernest A. Chilton, The Macmillan Company

12. Drawing by Richard Dorman, Office Building, Dorman/Muirselle Associates

13. Drawing by Jim Hamilton, Seattle Center Hospital, Fred Bassetti & Company, Architect

14. Architects/Planners Alliance, Inc., Ralph F. Evans Architect, Developer, Owner

15. *The Metaphorical Way of Learning and Knowing*, W.J.J. Gordon, Porpoise Books

16. Reprinted from the January 1977 issue of *Progressive Architecture*, copyright 1977, Reinhold Publishing Company, p. 72 (Richard L. Crowther)

17. "The Speechmaker's Quandry, Here's How Mark Twain Solved It", *Educational Dealer*, January/February 1977

18. Reprinted from the January 1977 issue of *Progressive Architecture*, copyright 1977, Reinhold Publishing Company, p. 68 (Burt, Hill & Associates)

19. Fiberglass/Plastic Design Guide, prepared by Owens-Corning Fiberglass Technical Center, Market Development Laboratory Design Department under the direction of J.A. Keown, illustrations by D.A. Damico

20. Timberform, Inc.

21. Reprinted from the September 1978 issue of *Progressive Architecture*, copyright 1978, Reinhold Publishing Company, p. 123

22. *Architectural Illustration of the Value Delineation Process*, Paul Stevenson Oles, AIA United States Pavilion Expo '67 (early scheme), R. Buckminster Fuller/S. Sadao

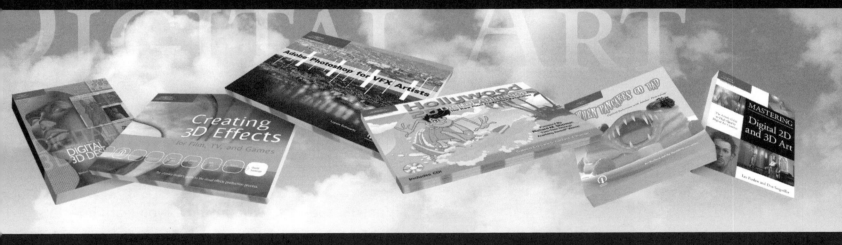